Footsteps My Journey

Kathy M. Hampton AKA Kathy Bee

This book is dedicated to the memory of Mary Stevenson, who God gave her the words and she just pushed the pen; to Don Hampton who helped me help Mary; and to everyone who loves the poem '**Footprints In The Sand**" Be Blessed Be A Blessing!

Kathy Bee Hampton & Mary Stevenson Zangare

CONTENTS

The Chorus Girl Mary Stevenson

PREFACE

Mary would always put on a pot of coffee and then share a story like a parable...to help you to receive a greater message. I begin with my favorite Mary Stevenson story...

It was the fall of 1942. A beautiful young woman, in her early twenties was lying on her bed painfully crying. Her black mascara had completely re-decorated the satin, pink, frilly bedspread. A crumpled-up letter was lying on the floor beside her. As the late afternoon sun, poured into her room, through doily-like curtains, sounds of hatred also filled the room. A herd of well-dressed women marched below her window, clanging cowbells and chanting "Sluts and whores you're going to hell…
listen to your tolling bell!"

She suddenly stopped crying as her eyes became focused on a small, pink, embroidered pillow. With trembling hands, she picked up the pillow and recited the written words "To Thine Own Self Be True!" Her mind raced back to the time when she had first embroidered those words. It was only a year ago. She had just landed a new job dancing in the Troc Burlesque Theater in Philadelphia and for the first time in her life, lived on her own in a "For Women Only" boarding house. She thought about how the men adored her and showered her with gifts, flowers and praises. She considered herself to be the ultimate, total, self-sufficient, woman, who needed no one! Then _he_ came along, the man of her dreams, Mr. Right. How was she to know that he had another life, a wife and kids?

Lying exposed on the bed was a cold, black, metal, object that had been hiding under the pillow. This small handgun was a special gift given to her from her father, when she left home, to begin her show-biz career. He said that it could protect her from harm. "How ironic," she thought. Now it can protect me from the ghosts of shame, hurt and pain that live in my head." Her hands trembled as she reached for the gun. A sharp knock at the door caused her to freeze.

"Linda are you in there?" a lady's voice sternly yelled.

Linda ignored the voice and again reached for the gun.
"Knock! Knock! Knock! "Linda I know you're in there! Let me in, I

need to talk to you!"

Linda reluctantly tossed the embroidered pillow over the gun, and then slowly walked to the door. She opened it to find the pretty, but frail, young blond dancer, from the chorus line, Mary Stevenson.

"What the hell do you want, Mary...my blood like everyone else? Can't you see, I'm not dressed to receive visitors?"
Linda's swollen eyes glared at Mary.

Mary threw open the door and quickly entered the room. The smell of alcohol perfumed the air like a brewery. She ran past the shocked-faced Linda, and pounced on Linda's blackened, tear soaked bed. Chants from the women outside the window could still be heard.

In a low, scratchy, voice, Mary piped, "I didn't come here to give you any of my advice. You probably know more about life then I do...Something told me...Uh.... I just felt like I should give you this." Mary placed a piece of paper, with hand scribbled words on it, on top of Linda's embroidered pillow. She walked over to Linda, pulled the stone-cold woman close and hugged her. No words were exchanged. Then she gave Linda a big smile, turned and walked out of the room.

Infuriated, Linda slammed the door behind her. "The nerve of that little witch... Who does she think she is?" Linda shouted. "She ain't nothin' but a sleazy show girl like me...at least that's what all those women out there are saying." Linda's tears started gushing down her face. "They don't know me...Marty was the first man that I'd ever known. I loved him. He said he wanted to marry me. He never told me he was married and had kids. Now he's back with them and I'm left here all alone. I don't want to live anymore." Linda reached again for the gun, but her hands betrayed her and picked up the paper, Mary had left behind.

Her eyes slowly began reading the words:

One night I had a dream I was walking
Along the beach with the Lord.
Many scenes from my life flashed across the sky.
In each scene I noticed FOOTPRINTS in the sand.

Often times there were two sets of footprints
However I noticed that during the most trying periods of my life

> When I was suffering from anguish, sorrow or defeat
> There was one set of FOOTPRINTS only.
> This bothered me. So I said to the Lord,
> You promised me Lord that if I followed You,
> You would walk with me always.
> Why Lord, when I needed you most,
> You had not been there for me?
> The Lord replied, the times when you have seen,
> Only one set of FOOTPRINTS in the sand,
> Is when I carried you.

With tear-filled, joyful eyes, lifted up toward the sky, Linda moaned then whispered, "Thank you God, thank you."

Two weeks later, Mary Stevenson had just finished her first big solo dance number. Admirers and awe-struck fans gathered around her. Linda squeezed through the crowd and handed Mary a note, then turned and walked away. Perplexed, Mary wiped off the perspiration from her face and opened the note. It read:

Mary, come to my room. I've got something to show you.
After graciously thanking her new patrons, Mary promptly appeared at Linda's door. This time she was greeted with a smile and a hug. Linda led Mary over to her stain-free bed, and pointed to a small white-laced embroidered pillow. The words on the pillow were Mary's own God given words, **FOOTPRINTS IN THE SAND.**

"This is so I can sleep on God's words every night." Linda proudly announced.
Mary smiled and touched the pillow. She had nothing to say. A feeling of peace and tranquility filled the room.
Then Linda gently clasped Mary's hand in hers and openly confessed, "Mary your words saved my life. Thank you!" Mary humbly replied, "God gave me the words, I just pushed the pencil."

Throughout my 20 years with Mary Stevenson Zangare, she would share many stories with me...not all in one setting. In fact, only if I needed the lesson that could be derived from the moral of the story... Of the many stories that Mary told, that of "The Chorus Girl" was one of my favorites...

But let's begin when I first met Mary...

1 THE PROMISE

What an exciting thrilling time in my life. I was twenty-four and thought I had the world by a string. After two years of singing with my own band **Santa Fe Junction & Kathy Bee,** throughout the South and Mid-west, I landed the opportunity to record with the world renowned **Steve Miller Band**. For years, I enjoyed their hit songs including, **FLY LIKE AN EAGLE, THE JOKER, and ROCK'N ME**. Their financial manager, Jay Rosenthal discovered my vocal talent in San Angelo, Texas, and then proceeded to make arrangements for me to sing with the ultimate band in…CALIFORNIA! I was elated! All my life, I wanted to be in California. I couldn't wait to meet the people, sing in the recording studios, and audition for musical plays. This was a dream come true!

Newly acquire friend, Bill, provided the living quarters while my husband, Jim and I waited for the recording session date. During our first week in town, Bill made arrangements for me to sing at the infamous **PALOMINO CLUB** in North Hollywood. Willie Nelson, Linda Rondstadt, Merle Haggard, plus many other well-known Country artists had graced this very stage. Being originally from a small town in Ohio, I felt that an opportunity to sing in Hollywood, California, would be the career break I certainly needed.

For my Hollywood debut, I carefully chose a long flowing yellow and black chiffon gown, which accented my 22-inch waistline. Immediately, I realized that I was over dressed for the occasion. The sight of blue jeans and the smell of smoke and stale beer quickly gave it away. Even saw dust and peanut shells covered the floor. I looked like Cinderella, going to a ball and stuck out like a sore thumb.

"It doesn't matter how I look," I thought. "I'm here to sing, regardless of my inappropriate attire!"

The lights were low and the noise level matched the size of the large crowd. 6'4" Jim seemed to tower over everyone. This was to our advantage, for in no time he spotted empty seats, for our party of five, in the back of the room. A long eternity seemed to go by before I finally heard MC, Country Celebrity Cliffy Stone announce my name, "And now folks, all the way from Dallas, Texas, Miss Kathy Bee!"

"Texas, I'm from Bloomingburg, Ohio!" I mumbled, as I made my way through yards of cowboy wanna bees. My beautiful gown swept the floor and soon quickly became soiled with dirt and peanut shells as I made my way to the stage.

"You don't have to put yourself through this embarrassment." I expressed under my breath. Then suddenly my ears were pieced by a deep loud voice.

"Hey what song are you gonna sing?" The guitar player curtly barked.

With total confidence, I answered, "**Blue Bayou** in the key of B-flat."

The entire band looked amazed, as the bass player spouted "I don't believe it, a chick singer who actually knows her key."

As the song began, with the familiar bass guitar introduction, I felt the words smoothly, easily flow out of my mouth, until I held the very last high note. The crowd clapped and roared. Then the band proceeded to shake my hand and ask for my business card. "But I don't have a card." I confessed. "I don't even have a permanent California address." I smiled and said.

As I turned and walked off the stage I whispered, "What I do have is pure satisfaction that the audience liked <u>my</u> performance!"

All of a sudden, people began to surround me and bestow upon me so many greetings and compliments, that it made the simple act of returning to my seat, a time consuming ordeal. At the very moment that I became reunited with my seat, I felt a light tap on my shoulder. Slowly I turned and saw a heavyset, middle aged, lady, sporting a beautiful smile.

"My name is Mary Stevenson Zangare" she announced. "I'm a descendent of Robert Louis Stevenson and I think you have a fantastic voice! **BLUE BAYOU** is one of my favorite songs."

I politely thanked her and without missing a beat, she continued to talk. Her blue eyes gleamed as she carried on about the entertainment business and how she had been a dancer in the Follies. Then all of a sudden, Mary began tap dancing. I nervously glanced over at my friends, who were staring at her, in astonishment. Finally, when the song ended, she finished dancing, followed by a silent unnerving hush. Instinctively, I began clapping my hands and thankfully the others joined in, providing Mary with the applause that she was definitely seeking.

I couldn't help but wonder if this lady was crazy or just eccentric. Breathless and panting, Mary then let out a low, gruff, infectious laugh that caught on like wild fire. Soon everyone was laughing. After the laughter died down, I invited Mary to join us and we spent the rest of the evening swapping Show Biz stories. At the close of the evening, as we rose to say our good-byes, Mary grabbed my hand and asked if I liked spaghetti? Emphatically, I answered yes, thinking anyone who's ever been on the road, loves a good home cooked meal.

The very next week, Jim and I found ourselves at Mary's home for a spaghetti dinner. As we drove up, we spied a small little house in a quiet mom and pop neighborhood. The front yard was overwhelmed with bushes and bright flowers. This view alone somehow reflected Mary's bright personality, making you want to automatically smile.

A robust man with a warm smile greeted us at the door, "You must be Kathy Bee and Jim," He announced. "Mary hasn't stopped talking about you since she heard you sing in Hollywood. I'm Basil, her husband. Come right in and make yourselves at home."

Immediately, I noticed Mary's entranceway walls, where most people hung family pictures, she hung plaques, accommodations, framed poems, pictures of U.S. Presidents and other dignitaries. I was especially drawn to a poem mounted on a plaque that had a figurine of a baby attached to the bottom. As Jim followed Basil into the living room, at the end of the hallway, I stood still and I read the words to the poem.

THE LITTLE SEED
I was just a little seed, no one knew me at all
But then I blossomed in a pouch and was born
Sometime in the fall
Everything was doing fine, until one day I really cried

I got beat so badly I couldn't talk
And nowhere could I hide
I stopped crying scared with fright.
What could the matter be?
I couldn't sleep; I couldn't eat.
And why do they beat me?
They say us children, we don't know
Because we are too small
Pain is not a way of life. Can love conquer all?
Lord, turn the wheel around; punish them that punish us
Because we are so tiny,
We didn't know we made such a fuss...
So send us to the ones who care
And will raise us as their own
And every time we cry and scream,
They'll love our every tone.
Written by Mary Zangare

Raw emotions arose in me and my eyes instantly began to water. I looked around for Mary and spotted her nearby in her old-fashioned kitchen stirring spaghetti sauce. The area resembled a battle zone with unorganized pots and pans everywhere. Slowly, I walked toward her and gave her a big bear hug. I could hardly get the words out, "Mary your poem, **THE LITTLE SEED** is beautiful."

Mary pleasingly replied, "You like that? Well I've got lots more of those, where that came from. Wait here." In a whirl, Mary was out of the kitchen and back again. In her arms, she carried a big brown box. With one big swoop, she dumped out a pile of poems, onto the kitchen table. I was in awe. There lay before me hundreds of large and small pieces of paper, some handwritten, some typed. Intently, I read through about twenty poems when I noticed an old yellowed, piece of paper. On it was the handwritten words to **FOOTPRINTS IN THE SAND** dated 1939.

Those familiar words had always been with me. My mom gave me a copy of it, when I first went on the road with my band and I carried it everywhere. I wondered, "Why did Mary have such an old copy of this poem? Could she too, be a fan of **FOOTPRINTS?"**

Mary, Jim and Basil's booming voices could easily be heard laughing away in the adjoining living room. As I entered the room, I quickly caught Mary's eye and motioned for her to join me in the kitchen. Instantly she leaped through the doorway, "What's up kid?" She joyously asked.

"Why do you have this old copy of **FOOTPRINTS IN THE SAND?** It's one of my favorite poems. My mom gave me a copy of **Footprints** on a little card when I first went on tour with the Flowers Family group. Is it one of your favorites too?" I curiously inquired.

"No," Mary sternly replied. "It's not one of my favorite poems...even though I did write it."

Perplexed, I proceeded to set her old copy of **FOOTPRINTS** down, then rapidly dug into my purse and showed her my copy that had a portrait of Jesus printed on the other side .

"But how could you have written it...when it says here, Author Unknown?" I strongly insisted as I presented Mary with my copy.

Mary became very serious. A sad look appeared on her face as she picked up her old worn-out copy of **FOOTPRINTS** and seated herself in a nearby chair.

After what seemed like an eternity of silence, Mary spoke, "I wrote this poem when I was a young girl." My mother died of tuberculosis, when I was six and daddy was left to care for the six of us kids. We had a hard, hard life. The Depression of the 30's was tough on everyone. Even though daddy loved us and tried his best, we had very little to eat. He was a stevedore, who worked on the Delaware River near our home in Chester, Pennsylvania. When he was home the refrigerator was full of food. But when he left for work, a week later, we were eating the paint off the walls and the tar off of roof. My oldest sister Helen used to line us up and ration the little bit of leftover food. Then we'd drink water to try and trick our stomachs into thinking that it had just finished a great big meal. Although it was tough, we respected and loved each other.

I was the black sheep of the family...always in trouble. I hated school because the kids frequently teased us about being diseased. They thought that they could catch tuberculosis from us, since it killed our mother. They also teased us about the way we dressed. I only owned two dresses, one was for school and the other was for church. But we were always clean and honest.

When I was fourteen, I decided I wasn't going to school anymore. The harder daddy tried to make me go, the harder I fought him. One time he walked me to the front steps of the schoolhouse and I turned around and walked out the back door. We constantly fought until I eventually wore him down. He gave up and allowed me to quit school. How I regret that, to this very day." I remember him saying "Stevey?" "That was his pet name for me." Mary proudly remarked. "What do you intended to do with the rest of your life?"

I boldly swore that I was going to become a famous dancer, then a movie

star and then a poet like our descendant Robert Louis Stevenson. Daddy
shook his head saying, "Stevey only dead poets make money."

I piped, "I don't want to make money, I just want to help other people!"

"It was a freezing cold morning, in December of 1936, when I found
myself locked out of the house. My younger sister Dot was at school, dad
was at work and I had forgotten my keys. After trying all the secured
windows and doors, I became exhausted and sat down on the snow
covered porch steps, shivering. I thought about how warm it was in the
schoolhouse. Then I thought about my mother, up in heaven with God.
If she had not died, she would have been home right now, baking bread
and cookies. I really missed her. What a beautiful woman she was...a
concert pianist, from a wealthy family. Mother would often play at parties
and social events, while father would join her, singing some of the most
popular songs of the day. He had a wonderful Irish tenor voice. But after
mother died, his desire for singing died too."

"I thought about how I had disappointed my father by dropping out of
school. The other kids excelled, while I was nothing but a quitter. How I
longed to make up for the hurt I saw in his eyes, on the day my mother
died and when my older brother Nelson, accidentally died...by falling off a
bridge and drowning. We were so young, yet I remember how much we all
cried, especially daddy. He walked around for months with the saddest
look in his eyes. On the day I quit school, he gave _me_ that same sad look.
I felt so ashamed.

I thought about all the misery and sorrow there had been in my life. Was
it always going to be this bad? So I looked up at God and pleaded "Am I

always going to be the one who messes everything up, the fool, the idiot? Please God, I love you and I've always believed in you. Many people are in pain, just like daddy and me. Give me something special that I can give to others."

"That's when I noticed the neighbor's cat majestically prancing by me, leaving his **FOOTPRINTS** in the snow." Mary's eyes joyfully danced as her hands imitated the frolicking cat. "In flash words appeared in my mind!" She exclaimed. "Thank God, I always carried pencil and paper. I quickly began writing the words that were in my head, down on paper. First I wrote: **One night I dreamed, I was walking in the snow with the Lord...** Then I abruptly stopped writing and began to shudder.

"Lord, I don't even like the cold snow" I complained. Immediately I began thinking of a much warmer place, a happier time. Images of sunshine and summer and my favorite places started swirling in my head. Then I saw the ocean. That's when an inner voice, God's voice gave me the words to **FOOTPRINTS IN THE SAND**!

I made copies for everyone. One time, **FOOTPRINTS** even saved a young dancer's life." Mary was smiling. An aura of warmth and goodness seemed to surround her.

I felt so ashamed that I had even questioned this lady. Totally captivated, I asked, "Why didn't you let the world know that you wrote **FOOTPRINTSIN THE SAND**? That you were the true author?"

Her overwhelming joy quickly turned to dismay as she replied "I tried. Years ago, one of our neighbors came over, and like you, began reading through my box of poems. After she read **FOOTPRINTS**, she scoffed "You copied that poem from someone else!"

"What do you mean?" I replied, not believing my own ears.

She scolded "I was at the local drug store and picked up a copy of **FOOTPRINTS** that was signed "**Anonymous**".

At first I didn't believe her. I asked Basil to take me to the same drug store and there was my poem, on a greeting card signed "Anonymous". My hands trembled and giant tears ran down my face as I handed the card to Basil. He sadly shook his head. I remember crying all the way home. I kept saying "How could someone do this to me? I'm not anonymous. I exist...I exist..."

"Mary," I softly interrupted, putting my hand on hers, "Why on earth didn't you and Basil take legal action?"

"We tried," her quivering voice lowered, almost to a whisper. "A friend of ours told us about an attorney who handled family law. The attorney informed us that he could do nothing for us. He then announced that **FOOTPRINTS** was probably in Public Domain by now and would probably cost thousands of dollars, to try and reclaim the poem. And Kathy, we had no money."

Mary whispered, "Basil often gets sick. We live on...disability. If God wants others to enjoy my poem then that's the way it's gotta be."

In my heart, I felt sorry for her. "Somehow people had to find out the truth," I thought to myself. With Mary's hand in mine, I promised "I'll help you get the word out that you Mary Stevenson Zangare are the true author of **FOOTPRINTS IN THE SAND!"**

Mary laughed and held up a finger in the air vowing "And I'm telling the world about my singing friend Kathy Bee! Kid we're gonna be famous together!"

We laughed until we were both crying! Basil and Jim wondered what was going on. None of us realized that this was just the beginning of a very long journey.

1939 Copy of Footprints In The Sand by Mary Stevenson

2 IT'S SHOW TIME

A month later, Jim found a job and we settled down into our own apartment. A week later, I awoke with a very queasy feeling in my stomach. I nudged Jim and told him it was time for work then tried to go back to sleep. The night before was a late one for me because I had landed a job singing with a Country Club group. We played Thursday through Saturday nights, to one of the toughest audiences that I had ever met. I had become accustomed to the warm hospitality that we received while playing in Texas and Oklahoma. Once again, a nauseating feeling hit hard and I ran for the bathroom.

Jim laughed "Do you think you might be pregnant?"

"How could I be?" I snarled. "We've only been married for five years and nothing has happened yet!"

"It's probably all of this California fresh, smoggy air. It probably made you fertile." Jim taunted.

Jim was right. I was pregnant.

Mary and I talked to each other at least two times a week. She was thrilled about my pregnancy. I was not. I wanted to leave California and be back on the road with my band.

One day, out of the blue Mary announced that she had made arrangements for us to perform at The Sahara Hotel in Las Vegas at a talent night hosted by Buddy Hacket's son, Sandy.

For three days in a row, I went to Mary's home and helped her develop a new routine. I told her that she could be the female version of Country Star, Grandpa Jones, (whom I adored). I dressed her in an old ladies' dress with a raggedy shawl, put her hair up in a bun, and sprayed it gray. We found a cane and some old-fashioned shoes. Then diligently we worked on her act, timing and jokes.

One week later, Jim and I were on our way to Las Vegas. First we stopped to get Mary and pleaded with Basil to join us.

"You kids go and have fun," He laughingly replied. "I'll have a pot of hot coffee and spaghetti waiting for you when you return."

Next, we headed down Interstate 15, in our gas guzzling Cadillac. Mary made the lunch, providing the best tasting tuna, cheese and onion sandwiches that I had ever consumed. After five long hours, through the boring desolate desert, without warning, large hotels sprang into view. Finally, we had arrived in Las Vegas.

Although Mary was a frequent visitor to Las Vegas and liked staying downtown, I found it a bit dirty and seedy...but exciting. This was my first Las Vegas experience. The sounds from the casinos, were heard everywhere. Money was dropping in trays. Alarms were going off. There was music, singers, dancers, people talking, shouting and yelling. During the day, it resembled a dust bowl but at night the place was transformed into a wonderland of beautiful lights.

Mary enjoyed playing the nickel and penny slots. I tried my luck at a dollar machine and to my total surprise, I won $100.00 jackpot on my third try.

Well, needless to say, I was hooked. (In Ohio, we never had games like those.) However, to be successful in Vegas, there were two major requirements.

#1. You had to be lucky.

#2. You had to have plenty of money.

The three of us had little luck and little money. But like idiots, we played all night with a show to do the next afternoon. At 6:00 AM Mary, Jim and I finally went to our rooms. At noon, Mary knocked on the door and one-hour later we were headed to The Sahara Hotel. Our strategy was "To become famous and let the world know about **FOOTPRINTS."**

Sandy Hacket, our MC was not kind to us. He swore at everyone, "Bitch move over here. You *bleep, bleep, bleep* you move over there."

I thought, how disrespectful. Who raised this spoiled child?

The hustle and bustle backstage was exhilarating. There were a variety of performers from comedians, singers, and dancers, all in a colorful array of costumes. Everyone's goal was to impress the agents and get a better gig. Soon the words "its show time" rang backstage. Like magic, the voices deadened to a silent hush. Then Sandy yelled out "Get your "bleep bleeps" ready. I quietly stood in the wings and watched the Elvis impersonator go on before me. Then I glanced around looking for Mary and spotted her chatting with a young dancer.

Finally my name was announced. I hurried onto the stage, handed the piano player with a copy of the sheet music to **THIS MASQUERADE** then walked to the center of the stage and waited for the piano introduction. From head to toe, I was draped in black, including a black cowgirl hat. Even the song that I had chosen had a dark meaning, which reflected my unhappy mood and current outlook on life:

ARE WE REALLY HAPPY HERE
IN THIS LONELY GAME WE PLAY
LOOKING FOR WORDS TO SAY, SEARCHING BUT NOT
FINDING UNDERSTANDING ANY WAY, WE'RE LOST IN
THIS MASQUERADE.

When I sang my last note, the audience showed their appreciation, by giving me a lengthy applause. I bowed thanked them, and then hurried backstage. Mary greeted me with a hug and remarked that she was so proud of me, assuring me that I would get many bookings from the various agents who were in the crowd.

Soon the name Stevey Stevenson was called.

Mary announced, "Oh that's me!"

I looked at her in bewilderment. "Who's Stevey Stevenson?"

"Oh that's the name my daddy called me!" Mary replied as she rushed to the stage.

"Break a leg Stevey!" I yelled!

Quickly, I found a spot, in the wings, where I could see Mary and observe the audience. She crept out on the stage doubled over like a ninety-year-old great-grandma. Then she used a trembling (old lady) voice, yet distinctly enunciated every word, to enhance her perfectly timed jokes and clown-like gestures. In no time, Mary completely won over the audience. After she'd finish a joke, on cue, she would straighten up her body, a fraction of an inch more. By the time she told her final joke, she was standing completely upright. Then Mary threw down her cane, took off her shawl and yelled to the band "Hit it boys!" Her 200-pound-plus body shimmied and shook, tapped and pranced to the song **SWEET GEORGIA BROWN**. When the band came to the final turn around, Mary kicked up both her heels and tapped wings, perfectly.

The crowd went wild. They were standing on their feet, clapping wholeheartedly. Mary, Stevey, Stevenson, Zangare received a Las Vegas standing ovation!

After the show, agents and impressed fans surrounded us as we collected numerous business cards. Even Sandy Hacket said congratulations and invited us to come back, anytime.

After the hoopla, Mary, Jim and I got something to eat. All through dinner, and during the drive back to California, we talked about the showcase. Mary proclaimed that it was one of the greatest Show Biz moments of her life.

"Until now," she smiled and said, "I basically gave up on being in show biz. I thought that my dancing career was over and that God wanted me to help the up and coming artists get their foot-in-the-door."

"Who knows what God has in store for you, Mary?" I gleefully chanted. "By the way, did you tell any of the agents that you were the author of **FOOTPRINTS**?"

Mary's mood instantly became sober. "I did, but I don't think they believed me."

Immediately, silence struck. I didn't know what to say. I thought to myself, "Was it too difficult for people to believe that a dancer could be close to God? Did people think that only certain types of people could be God's messengers?"

Mary patted my arm. "Basil said to me, when you first walked into our door, that you were the best person that I had <u>ever</u> brought home with me. Then he said "That girl will stick by you Mary and be a great help to you in the future."

I timidly smiled while feeling particularly uncomfortable. I thought. "What the heck did Basil mean by that?" It really bothered me.

"Do you know how I learned to dance?" Mary interrupted my thoughts.

"No, how did you learn Mary?" I wearily replied. I was feeling tired and sleepy after all the excitement of the day. My eyes could hardly remain open.

"I told you that we were poor and that we had no money." I slowly shook my head in agreement.

She continued, "The black kids taught me how to dance. We were friends and neighbors. Ethel Waters the famous movie star lived down the street and often reminded me to say, "please and thank you," for the cookies she baked us. Our next-door neighbor was a black lady named Mrs. Johnson and her cousin was Duke Ellington. When he'd come to town, we'd block off the streets, roll out the piano and have a huge Block Party.

Usually the colored kids (as they were known back then) and I danced on the street corners for money. They called me **WHITE CRACKER!** "Dance **WHITE CRACKER** Dance!" People yelled as they threw money at our feet. This money helped feed our families." A sorrowful look came over Mary's face. "I'll never forget what it felt like to suffer from starvation. The awful agony and pain you feel is intolerable and that memory sticks with you your entire life."

Silence filled the air again. Wide eyed, I looked back at Mary. She was staring out the car window. Quickly she turned around and stared at me, "I'm working on my life story and I'm going to call it **WHITE CRACKER**."

Sheepishly, I glanced over at Jim, who had not uttered a word, the entire drive home. He quickly glanced back and gave me a John Candy "Is this lady for real?" kind of smile.

We finally settled down and all became quiet, except for the sound of the car engine purring. I looked back at Mary. She had a peaceful look on her face. I studied her as she continued to look out the window. I could only imagine what she was thinking. Maybe she was reminiscing about other shows, other times, years ago. Or maybe she was thinking about...her book **WHITE CRACKER**...I didn't bother to ask. She looked too happy!

Two weeks later, Mary called. I could tell by the emotion in her voice that she was ecstatic, "Kathy, I've just landed a job as the MC and comedian at this club. I work Friday and Saturday nights, making $50.00 a night. This money will really come in handy supplementing our social security check. I want you to sing on our talent showcase next Saturday night."

"Sure, I'd love to." I replied. Mary gave me all the details. The following week, Jim and I stopped by her house, so that she could ride with us. She was having trouble with her equilibrium, which affected her driving. When we pulled in front of the house we notice a new red Firebird.

Mary opened the door and I was floored. I was expecting her to look like the old grandma character that brought the house down at The Sahara. Instead, she had her hair cut, colored and a new perm, wore a bright red and silver metallic looking blouse, topped off with huge earrings. Instantly she gave us a hug and invited us in.

"Nice car." Jim commented. "And expensive...Is that yours?"

"Oh no that belongs to my son." Mary blushed. "Basil and I bought it for him, when he was in high school. I've got to get my sweater."

Mary sweetly smiled then rushed into her bedroom.

As we waited for her to return, Jim looked at me and quietly asked, "I thought you said Mary and Basil lived on a small pension or on social security or something?"

"That's what she told me." I quietly responded.

"Then how could they afford to get their kid an expensive car like that?" He questioned.

I shrugged my shoulders in bewilderment. In no time Mary rushed back and off we went to the nightclub.

Upon entering the club, I instantly detected the smell of stale cigarettes. I hated it, but bars and cigarettes seemed to somehow always go together, especially in the late 70's. Throughout the room, the colors red and black were used to decorate the walls, furniture and the carpet. On a nearby bulletin board was posted my publicity picture, and below it hung Mary's glamorous, photo.

Without warning, Mary hurried past us and headed directly for the club owner. Jim gave me a peculiar look as we headed for some seats. Immediately, he spotted the perfect table, in the middle of the room, where the speakers wouldn't be too loud and in no time we were "nursing drinks" and watching the room fill-up with customers.

"Mary did so well in Vegas, at the Sahara, with her grandma routine…Why didn't she stick with that look…that was part of her act! You were there! You saw her. She was great" I ranted.

"I don't know." Jim remarked. "Maybe she wanted to be glamorous like she had been in the early days."

I shook my head and silently hoped that she could pull off this new routine. We had practiced the other act for days and it was successful.

Mary shortly returned, out-of-breath and annoyed. "The owner says he's too busy to meet you!"

"Don't worry about it Mary. I'll meet him when he has the time. When do I go on...what time?" I asked.

"Oh, you're the fourth act right after my friend Johnny Knight the Elvis impersonator." Her demeanor changed as her face lit up. "You've got to hear Johnny. He's great. And my son Andy plays the drums in his band. I'll go get them."

In no time Mary was back with two apprehensive-looking men on each side of her. Johnny was tall, with Elvis-styled black dyed hair and side burns. Andy was much shorter, thin and looked nothing like Mary. We asked them to join us. They pull-up chairs and sat while Mary did all the talking until the familiar words were yelled by the club owner "It's Show Time".

Andy was the drummer in the house band that also consisted of a bass guitar, lead guitar and a keyboard player. As the house lights dimmed, the stage lights lit-up the band and Mary. The owner, with mike in hand, announced,

"And now ladies and gentlemen, we are pleased to bring you, all the way from Las Vegas, Grandma Marty!"

"Grandma Marty, who the heck is that?" I wondered as I quickly glanced around the room.

Then flippantly he handed the microphone to Mary AKA Grandma Marty, who nervously proceeded to greet the audience, speaking so softly that you could scarcely comprehend what she was saying.

I couldn't believe it. This couldn't be the same lady who got the standing ovation from one of the toughest audiences in the world. She was bombing. I felt so embarrassed for her.

Later on, I sang a couple of songs and was received very well. But I couldn't get my mind off of Mary. It was like day and night. She definitely had an off night. I began to wonder if Mary and the owner got into an argument before the show? What set her off?

Two weeks later, Mary called and sadly reported that the club owner hired another MC.

"That's show biz." I reminded her while attempting to cheer her up.

"There are always more gigs out there. You'll see!"

Mary softly replied, "Maybe not for me." She chanted in almost a whisper. "Kathy, don't you ever give up on your dreams. Listen to this."

MAKE EVERY DREAM LAST

To believe in a dream that will never come true

Is a dream in itself when your chances are few?

Singers and dancers that never do make it

Actors they all share a dream and can't shake it

Someday, they keep hoping, somehow and when

If a big moment comes, will it fall through again?

For I'm getting older and wrinkling fast

Believe in your dreams and make every dream last.

Mary Zangare

Mary AKA Stevey The Entertainer

3 IT'S WHO YA KNOW KID

California was a very foreign place to me. In general, people did not seem to be very friendly. Maybe it was because rents were so high and it took everybody in the household to make a living, so you had no time to get to know your neighbors. My landlady, Marilyn and her husband Wayne and their four kids had adopted Jim and I. They were originally from Buffalo, New York and sympathized with my yearning for neighborly companionship. My own hometown of Bloomingburg, Ohio had 500 people in it and most of them were relatives. I missed my family and friends from high school.

My body was changing expanding and so were my emotions. Although Mary and I spoke frequently, over the phone and would visit each other at least once a week, I wanted someone closer to my age to talk to. I missed the times that we had on the road with the band. Oh how I missed Gary, Carl, Dave and Robert. We had been a family. Those guys were great musicians. "If only we hadn't come to stupid California and I hadn't gotten pregnant." I spouted to myself.

It was a typical sunny California day. An array of flowers bloomed and Palm trees (that served no useful purpose in my mind) swayed. The temperature was a perfect 75°. Every day the weather remained the same. Unlike the weather, I was making some major changes in my life. I concluded that I was going to do something different. My resolution was to quit feeling sorry for myself, walk up to the first stranger that I met and start up a conversation. As I walked out the door, I spotted a woman in her early thirties, who had long dark hair tied up in a bun. She was intently stripping some ugly, horrid, green, chipped, paint off of an antique chair. I stuck out my chest (and my little belly) strolled up to her and announced "Hi my name is Kathy Bee. What's yours?"

She looked up at me with a shocked expression. "Well...I'm Jackie White." Immediately, she took off her gloves and shook my hand. Still in a shocked state she blurted out, "You must not be from around here."

Surprisingly, I smiled and replied, "No, I'm originally from Ohio..."

"Hey! I'm your neighbor" she chuckled.

"Yeah," I thought to myself. "I can see that you're my neighbor and that you live right across from me."

She quickly noticed the strange look on my face, "Oh, I mean, I'm from Pennsylvania...and Ohio and Pennsylvania are neighboring states."

Jackie invited me in for some of her famous "sun tea". Her apartment was laid out in the same manner as mine except she had green carpet, compared to our orange. I sat on the couch nearby, and tried to figure out an unusual smell, that hovered throughout the room. Jackie went into the kitchen for the tea. As I looked around the room, I began to surmise that the two of them were only renting temporarily, since the room was packed with oversized furniture and decorations.

Soon Jackie returned and served the tea. We easily conversed exploring a wide range of subjects. Her husband David was a microbiologist and they met in Arizona during their college years. Although Jackie was currently working for a temporary agency, as a secretary, her dream was to become an agent or a screenwriter in Hollywood.

"Wow we had something in common," I thought. "I want to get my recording career going and Jackie wants to get into the movie business."

All of a sudden, a fat fuzzy creature hopped through the room and into the kitchen.

"What the heck was that?" I squealed.

Jackie laughed "Oh that's Maurice, our French Lop Ear rabbit. Isn't he just adorable?"

When I regained my composure, I quickly searched around the room and asked if Maurice had any buddies?

"Oh yes," she arrogantly professed. "David has an albino ferret…he lives in a cage. He would kill poor Maurice if he somehow managed to get a hold of him. They're natural enemies you know…but they're like our kids. When your baby is born, she will have two fuzzy playmates."

I thought, "Like heck she will."

Jackie ran into the kitchen and came back with the fat, 20-pound Maurice. She told me how she wanted to be his agent and get him discovered by the studios in Hollywood.

"He could be the rabbit version of Lassie." She seriously announced as she placed him on my lap. This creature began sniffing my leg as to say,

"Where's the beef or the carrots". I gently and most carefully picked him up and handed him back to Jackie.

"Oh he won't bite," she snapped.

I thought, "He's not going to get the chance." After closely studying Jackie and Maurice, I came to the conclusion that, this woman was <u>serious</u>. I further surmised, "She really wants to get her rabbit employed in Hollywood... she's a bona fide <u>stage</u> mother to a rabbit. I should put down the tea, thank her and go home...or I could offer to help Jackie and Maurice get a gig?"

"Jackie," I pried, "What does Maurice do...tricks?"

She looked at me coldly, "My Maurice doesn't have to do anything. He's too cute!" she curtly replied.

Immediately, I stood up to leave and I casually mentioned that I would see what I could do to help her. With shoulders slumped and belly tucked in, I crept back to my apartment, shut and tightly secured my door. The next two days, I thought nothing more about Jackie and her rabbit. Then there was a knock on my door. There, stood Jackie holding a covered dish filled with freshly baked chocolate chip cookies.

She was smiling from ear to ear. "Maurice and I want you to have these. We appreciate you offering to help."

For a second I was taken aback, and then I remembered our previous conversation.

I welcomed her in and jokingly asked, "And where's Maurice?"
She gave me a serious look and haughtily announced, "He decided to stay at home."

Jackie and I spent the afternoon talking. I rationalized that Jackie was interesting and friendly. Maybe I could get use to this Maurice idea. Hey, if a no talent rabbit could make it in show biz, then there was hope for pregnant me.

Within the next week, Jackie combed through The Los Angeles Times Newspaper and lined Maurice and I up with our first audition, for **THE GONG SHOW**. Jackie played the piano, and I sang **MY "BUNNY" VALENTINE** to the tune of **MY FUNNY VALENTINE** to Maurice while he sat on my lap. The next week we got a call to audition for **THE $1.98 BEAUTY PAGEANT**. I was so embarrassed. I was four months pregnant and showing. I adamantly did not want to audition. Jackie pleaded with me that this might be the break that Maurice and I needed…you never know who's going to be watching.

That's what I was afraid of. In my past life…before California and being with child, I appeared on TV in Oklahoma City (interviewed by Mary Hart of now Entertainment Tonight Fame), in concert all over the country, opened for Bob Hope, Crystal Gayle, Grandpa Jones, The Oak Ridge Boys and now I was about to appear on a corny show, singing lullabies to a rabbit. Reluctantly, I allowed myself to endure this kind of humiliation;

however I informed Jackie that this audition was the last of its kind. There had to be a better way to get exposure.

When we arrived backstage for our audition, Jackie set Maurice down and he quickly hopped away. The room was full of movie star hopefuls who weren't impressed by a loose rabbit. Jackie crawled around on her hands and knees calling for Maurice. I felt like crawling underneath one of the tables and hiding from her along with Maurice. Maybe that rabbit was smarter than I had thought. At least, he had since enough to hide. Then a shrill scream was heard from the back of the room, followed by some vulgar, truck driver type swear words. Maurice had been found. He chewed through one of the future $1.98 Beauty Queen's prize gowns and needless to say she was hot.

By the time Maurice and I auditioned, Jackie was so upset that she dropped the sheet music on the floor, in the middle of the song and I finished singing to Maurice, without accompaniment. All the while the cameras kept rolling. To top that off I had to strut around in a bathing suit. (Jackie strapped me into hers because mine no longer fit.)

I felt so humiliated that my tan face stayed red, all the way home. Jackie didn't open her mouth. She knew that I was fuming. As soon as the car was parked in the carport, I ran to my apartment. I was too angry to cry. "Rabbit stew" I spouted, "I'll fix her, if she mentions that rabbit to me again, he's going in my stewing pot along with his owner, Jackie!"

"Ring Brrring" my phone began ringing off the hook. I wouldn't answer; thinking for sure it was Jackie. Then a thought struck me, "What if it's Jim calling from work?" After the tenth ring, I grabbed the phone and angrily yelled, "Hello!"

"Kathy," a familiar voice declared. "It's Mary. Is there something wrong?" I filled Mary's ears describing every detail of the "bunny incident". Instead of receiving sympathetic words...I heard an abundance of laughter. At first I was hurt. Mary couldn't stop laughing. Then I began to join in and laugh at the situation. It seemed that Mary had also auditioned for the **GONG SHOW** and was called back twice. The third time they called her, she wasn't able to make the audition. Basil had suffered a heart attack and was placed in intensive care.

"And I stayed right by his side." she declared.

Then a horrible thought crossed my mind. "Oh Mary," I fearfully asked. "What if they call me back again? I don't want to be on that stupid show!" I boldly announced. "Mary what can I do? I want to help Jackie, but I really don't want to be known as Maurice's sidekick!"

Mary chuckled, "Take your phone off the hook for a couple of days. As for Jackie, I've got a friend, whose uncle is in Show Business. I'll help her get her rabbit on TV. Hey kid, "It's who ya know!"

The next week, Mary came to the apartments and met Jackie and Maurice. When Mary learned that they were both from Pennsylvania, the two of them talked for hours. Ultimately, Mary promised Jackie that she would get Maurice a spot on the TV show **C.H.I.P.S.** (One of Mary's Las Vegas traveling buddies, Flo was the niece of the producer of **C.H.I.P.S**) In turn,

Jackie agreed that she would help Mary get a movie deal for her book, her autobiography, **WHITE CRACKER**.

Mary became motivated and completely dedicated to completing her book. "I want the world to know about poverty and suffering. I want them to read my poems…I've got so much to say." She proclaimed.

Then a month went by and I hadn't heard much from Mary or Jackie. I knew that they were both busy working together. Jackie found someone to type Mary's book, while Mary was working on her connections for Jackie. Two months later, late in the evening, the phone rang. It was Mary. "I did it! I did it!" she was chanting wildly.

"Did what?" I asked trying to decipher her words.

"I got Maurice on **C.H.I.P.S**. They start filming next week."

We chatted a little more then we hung up. I was wondering why Jackie hadn't said anything to me about the news. Maybe Mary hadn't informed her yet. The next day I knocked on Jackie's door. She invited me in but seemed obviously rushed. She was dressed in her Sunday best holding Maurice by a fancy dog chain hooked to a new dog collar.

"What's up?" I asked, "Are you going somewhere?"

"Maurice and I are off to Hollywood for his photo session. I've only got a few minutes to chat." She replied.

"When were you going to tell me about **C.H.I.P.S**?" I coldly asked.

"Oh that Mary," Jackie giggled. "I told her that I wanted to be the one to let you know, but she spilled the beans." Then Jackie quickly opened her front door as to say, "It's time to go now".

"If you're afraid that I want to be at the filming of **C.H.I.P.S**, Jackie…don't worry, I don't <u>want</u> to go!" I angrily responded and walked away.

I felt hurt and betrayed. All of a sudden, Maurice's sidekick wasn't even good enough to touch his fur. He was going to Hollywood to be a star and I…"Wait a minute" I told myself. "If a no talent, fat, rabbit can get into the movies, then what the heck is stopping me from succeeding in the music industry?" I felt a brand new wave of hope embrace me, big belly and all. The rabbit incident spurred me on to make some calls of my own. I had a few VIPs up my sleeve.

Maurice did appear on **C.H.I.P.S.** His segment dealt with animal cruelty. **C.H.I.P.S.** officers, Ponch and John drove up on their motorcycles and spotted Maurice left alone in a hot car, with the windows rolled up. The officers stormed into the nearby store and informed the pet owner that her <u>dog</u> could die from heat exposure. On the way out of the store, the lady repeatedly apologized to them, then reached in her car and handed them Maurice. They looked surprised when they saw that the dog was really a rabbit.

I hadn't had a chance to chat with Mary until days after the show. Mary explained that Jackie never informed her about **C.H.I.P.S** either. Mary's friend Flo told her about the taping then arranged for Mary to be on the set.

Mary chuckled. "You should have seen Jackie's face when I walked up behind her. You would have thought she had seen a ghost, as pale as she turned. By the way, Could you do me a favor?"

"What's that?" I curiously asked.

"Jackie promised to pay me a commission from Maurice's **C.H.I.P.S'** money, for getting them the gig. Could you remind her of that promise because I could really use the money?"

Even though I was pretty ticked about the entire ordeal, I recouped Mary's commission check, from Jackie. When I asked Mary about her book **WHITE CRACKER**, she assured me that it was completed but many things had been omitted and changed from her original notes. However, Jackie said that it was great and claimed to have placed it with Mary Tyler Moore.

"I love the name **WHITE CRACKER**," Mary expounded. It represents who I really am, and where I came from. I wrote a poem about being The **WHITE CRACKER**. Would you like to hear it?"

"Yes Mary." No sooner had the words escaped my mouth, Mary began quoting her poem.

THE WHITE CRACKER
I was called The WHITE CRACKER
By the blacks who helped raised me
I was dancing on the street corners,
By the early age of three

The love we shared for each other,

Surpassed our being poor

Living as sister and brother,

While surviving the poverty war.

I was called The WHITE CRACKER, from Chester, PA.

Dancing with black children for pennies and nickels a day.

Somehow we remained happy even when we had nothing to eat.

We were always clean and honest, no one did we ever cheat

We ate the plaster off the wall

And anything else we could.

We heated the house with the coal oil stove

Because we had no wood.

We cared deeply for each other; poverty we tried to shake.

Vowing when we all grew older,

A better world we'd try to make.

Now each and every step I take, I know Lord…You are near

And when my earthly journey ends,

Your words I hope to hear.

"My child you helped your brothers

And accomplished so much more

Your treasure's here in heaven…where

You will never again be poor.

Mary Zangare

I was amazed at the amount of poems, that must have been stored in her brain…yet only a few people knew of Mary Stevenson Zangare. "Kid It's who ya know." Those words kept replaying in my head. Mary was right. It's not always what you know…It's "who ya know, kid".

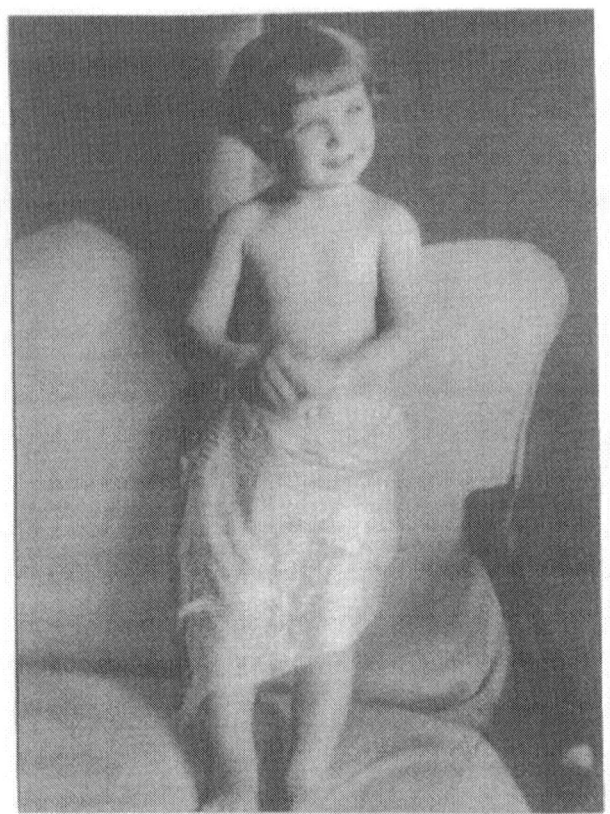

Mary at the age of three was later proud of the fact that
she danced on street corners, in order to help her family
during the Depression.

4 AND YOU CARRIED ME

Motherhood did not look good on me. As my swelling belly expanded, my show clothes became clown-like. The clientele, at the country club were taking bets, on when I was going to pop!

Mary and I kept in touch weekly. Mary's son, (fresh out of high school) and his young wife lived with Mary and Basil and were expecting their first child. Although Mary was thrilled about the idea of being a grandmother, again, she often spoke about how difficult it was for two grown women to live under the same roof.

During one of Mary's visits and over many cups of coffee, she shared with me stories about her early adulthood and her first pregnancy. Mary confessed that she had been married before; to her oldest son Andy's father, Tony and said they once lived with his mother.
"I met Tony at a dance. He appeared to have it all, nice clothes, a family that was well off, a good job, a car and extra money. When he asked me to marry him, I figured I had hit the jackpot…how young, naive and stupid!

We ran away and got married. I was only sixteen and had no idea what you were supposed to do. My father never discussed sex with any of us. (Sex was a taboo subject.) Tony rented a motel room for the night and informed me that we were supposed to sleep together, I was terribly offended.
"Good girls don't do that sort of a thing!" I shouted.

"He bent over laughing, "You're my wife Mary. You're allowed to sleep with me. That's what husbands and wives do." He asked me if I needed something to drink to relax me? I've never been a drinker. I couldn't stand even the smell of it but I told him that some liquor might help. When Tony left to buy the liquor, I crept out of the window, onto the fire escape and ran for a cab. I instructed the cabby to take me home, directly.

Once I arrived, the house was dark and everyone was asleep. As I had done on so many other occasions, I quietly climbed in the house, through my bedroom window. I shared the room with my little sister Dot, who was fast asleep. I was so overjoyed seeing my own bed, that I didn't even put on my pajamas…just jumped right in! The next morning my father was surprised to see me lying there. He had discovered through the "small town" grapevine that I ran off with Tony and got married."

He shook me and questioned, "Stevey where's your husband Tony?"

Still feeling drowsy from the night before, I casually answered, "Oh I left him because he wanted to sleep with me?"

After dad stopped chuckling, he sternly shook his head, and strongly suggested that I go back to my new husband. He told me that I had made my bed and now I had to lie in it! Reluctantly, I followed his instructions.

Mary's voice became raspy. She cleared it and proceeded. "I really tried to be the best wife ever. It was exceptionally painful and difficult. We lived with Tony's mother. She hated everything about me. Tony and his mother even hated my poetry. So, I secretly carried around with me a copy of **FOOTPRINTS**. Those words were a great comfort to me. Yet, with all that I was going through, it seemed like I had written them, a million years ago. I wasn't allowed to dance anymore because he maintained that I was making a spectacle out of myself and that I was an embarrassment to his entire family. When I found out that I was pregnant, Tony's mom informed Tony of our news, before I even returned home from the doctor's office.

I tried to please Tony and his family. I became a Catholic. I tried to be a better cook and housekeeper, but there was no pleasing Tony or his mother, so I decided to leave. I went home.

Tony came over every day, begging and pleading. He said that our baby deserved a father and promised that he would find us a home of our own. So he rented us a small apartment. I was impressed by his efforts and finally gave in. For a time, we were happy. I was at last able to functions as a wife. But before long he complained about my cooking. He often unfairly compared it to his mother's. Then he stopped eating at home and refused to even buy groceries. I was left pregnant, alone and starving, while he ate at his mothers.

Then he installed a dead bolt on the door and kept the key, locking me inside the upstairs apartment. The old familiar hunger pains visited me once more. I was becoming frail and sickly. Tony noticed my worsening condition and out of embarrassment, because my frail, skinny body, made him to look bad, in front of his friends, he gave me a quarter for a can of soup. This went on for months. My friends and my family passed me notes underneath the door. Tony would come home late at night and beat me.

Sometimes he alleged it was because he found dust on the furniture. If I cried too long, he'd lock me in the closet. I felt so sorry for the new little baby growing inside of me. I had to get away...but how? Feeling completely alone and helpless, I sat down at the table and spoke out loud to God, "You promised me that you would never leave me or forsake me.

Where are you now?" My mind immediately transported itself back to the ocean…to God's footprints. I closed my eyes and was suddenly swept off of my feet. Was this a dream…an illusion? Somehow I lost time. When I woke up, I was sitting on the kitchen floor. Words began forming in my head. I ran to the sink and grabbed a pencil then hurried into the bedroom and grabbed a clean sheet of paper…Rapidly I scribbled down the words that were still lingering:

AND YOU CARRIED ME

You carried me across the sand and to the mountaintop

Over every brush, every tree, and every single crop.

You showed me the great cities,

My hair gently blew in the breeze,

I wish that I could be like You

Then everyone Lord, I would please.

When we came down from the mountaintop

I noticed in Your eye a tear

You said, "I didn't want it to be this way

A world of hatred, chaos and fear.

So I wrote the Ten Commandments,

To let the whole world know

Regardless of race color or creed,

I will always love them so.

I must go now my child, to the land above the sea.

I surely will remember them, if they'll remember Me.

Mary Zangare

Mary stared deeply into my eyes. "Kathy, I felt completely cleansed. I had seen the entire world through God's eyes. I left my body and was taken to the mountaintop, with the Lord. When I returned, I knew that no <u>man</u> could ever harm my baby or me.... I would never forget my experience or those words." Then she cupped my hands in hers. "You once asked me what's my favorite poem? **And You Carried Me,** that's <u>my</u> favorite." tears begin to form in Mary's baby-blue eyes.

I felt a chill in my bones. "A unique spiritual experience had taken place in her life. This wonderful lady made my problems look exceptionally pint size. If God could carry Mary, then He could carry anyone." I thought to myself.

Abruptly, Mary released my hands, walked over to her gigantic purse and pulled out pad and pencil. "I'll make you a fresh copy of **And You Carried Me**. Would you like that?"

Dumbfounded, I nodded my head up and down like a toy puppy in the back of a car window.

She proceeded to speak. Simultaneously, without hesitation, she wrote the words to her poem while continuing her conversation. "Years later, one of my friends explained that the poem, And You Carried Me was the sequel to **FOOTPRINTS IN THE SAND**. I had no idea what the word "sequel" meant until she explained that it was the continuation of **FOOTPRINTS**. She was right. It was the sequel. There now, you have your own copy."

I took the poem and thanked her. Then nonchalantly checked the words of my new poem with her original…the words were exactly the same. Mary's brain was like some multi-track tape recorder.

Without missing a beat, Mary continued her story. "Tony made me feel like I was a prisoner. To pass the time, I would sing songs to the baby inside me, even though my voice was not the best and I continued to secretly write poetry. Due to the little nutrition that I received my body grew very weak.

One evening, my temperature soared through the ceiling. Tony came home and completely ignored my pleas to call the doctor. Instead he decided to take a shower but forgot to take his towel. We shared the bathroom, with the landlady who lived downstairs. When he yelled upstairs for me to bring his towel, I was aching and too sick to comply.
So I yelled back, "Tony I don't feel well. Can't you get the towel yourself?"

Like a tremendous bolt of lightning, he flew up the stairs and slapped me across the face. I lost my balance and fell down the flight of stairs, baby and all. The only thing that I remembered was cracking my head on the radiator, at the bottom of the stairs.

I woke up with a splitting headache. My blurred vision finally focused in on a familiar picture sitting on top of a piano. It was the picture of my mother, smiling down at me. I was home, at my father's house. Dad explained how Tony left me lying on the floor.

"He probably thought you were dead." He yelled. "I'll kill him to look at him!" Dad exploded. "If your landlady hadn't called...She told me to come and get you, because she didn't want a young girl dying in her house."

Our family doctor agreed that I had experienced a very close call with death. He shook his head in disgust when he viewed my malnourished pregnant body. A week later, the doctor was called again. Only this time it was to deliver my baby. Dad looked at me so proudly, "Well Stevey, you've got yourself a fine, healthy, little boy. "What are you going to name him?" Without hesitation, I answered, "Andrew...after you dad." God once again carried me safely home.

I thanked Mary for another great story...and then encouraged her to get a copyright on her poem. She agreed that this would be a great idea...

5 MY NATIVE AMERICAN FAMILY

The word was out, all over town, about Tony, the new baby and me. I feared that Tony would come looking for us. On a cold December morning in 1941, I wrapped up little Andy, in warm woolen blankets and took a train to Oklahoma. The plan was to stay with my aunt, who owned a boarding house.

I loved riding the train. The sound of the tracks was so soothing, even little Andy seemed to enjoy the ride. He was such a good baby, who never fussed and only cried when he was hungry. The song **WHITE CHRISTMAS** that frequently played on the radio was constantly serenading us. By the time we arrived in Claremore, Oklahoma, I knew all the words.

The weather had turned to blizzard-like conditions. With baby in one arm and my meager bag of clothing in the other, I set out, on foot, to find my aunt's house. I didn't even have enough money for a cab. What seemed like an eternity, half-frozen and hungry, we finally arrived at my aunt's door. I knocked...no answer. I knocked even louder and more frantically...no answer. Panicking, I looked up at the sky and at the top of my lungs shouted, "Lord what do I do now?"

A man walking by yelled back, "What did ya say lady?"

I was too cold to be embarrassed and yelled, "Where's the lady who owns this place? She's my aunt."

He screamed, "If you're lookin' for the owner of that place, she closed up shop and moved away, just about a week ago. I think they said she was movin' to Texas."

All of a sudden, I felt the blood rush cold, through my body. I was totally lost, doomed. Icy tears involuntarily streamed down my face and onto my frozen cheeks. I began haplessly walking in circles, until I came to a huge tree in a park. Glistening, snow softly hugged the ground, bushes, and trees resembling a scene from a fancy Christmas Card. Everything around me was covered in beautiful…pure white. Even though my body was numb, I took off my warm jacket and placed it around little Andy.

"It wasn't his fault that we were in this mess," I thought. Holding Andy tightly, I carefully sat down on the icy ground and rested by body against the big oak tree. Briefly, I closed my eyes. "Take me Lord to a warmer place," I chanted over and over as my teeth chattered like a typewriter in my head.

All at once there was a rustling sound, coming from the nearby bushes. As I opened my eyes, I noticed prints in the snow. These prints did not belonging to a cat. They were much larger. Out of nowhere, sprang a huge gray dog. Instinctively, I threw my entire body around Andy. "Lord, I'm too weak to fight," I thought. Then I noticed a warm look in the dog's eyes and that his long furry tail was wagging. He quickly snuggled up against Andy and me, like he was our long lost pet.

Then A peaceful feeling swept over me. My mind drifted off and I traveled back again to that warm familiar place in the sand. "God's **FOOTPRINTS** are carrying me," I thought as I fell into a deep sleep.

"Although my eyes were closed, I could hear strange voices. Was I dead? Was I dreaming? Was I in heaven? I even felt nice and warm. Slowly, as I opened my eyes, I saw a room full of tanned skin people, Native Americans. They were trying to figure out what to do with me. The leader emphatically was telling the others about how he had followed the **FOOTPRINTS** of a person and a wolf, in the snow. Then he found them under a tree lying together.

He said that the great wolf was very protective of the yellow-haired woman and small baby. At first, he wouldn't let him come near and then suddenly the wolf raced away. That's when he carried the woman and the child to the village not knowing if the woman was going to survive the night. I shot up like a cannon. "Where's my baby?" I screamed. "Where's little Andy?"

"Your baby is fine, little Yellow Hair," the leader assured me. "The wolf saved you and your son's life. His warm fur kept you from freezing to death. You have been blessed by the gods! Now you need to rest."

From that day on, I was known as Yellow Hair and Andy was named Little Eagle Feather.

We moved in with a heavy-set, stern-looking woman named Ruby Miles. She was full-blooded Cheyenne, with long black hair streaked with gray strands. When her husband had passed away two years prior, at his funeral service, she never shed a tear. This earned her the nickname Stone Face, the woman who never cries.

She instantly noticed the bruises and scars on my body. "When you feel like talking to me, I'll be here to listen," Ruby softly said.

Without warning, it felt like a dam had erupted inside me. I poured my heart and soul out to this attentive stranger, telling her every detail of the torturous ordeal that Tony put me through. I also let her know that he still could be trying to find us and that I was deathly afraid of him.

Although Ruby lived in a tiny two-bedroom red mud adobe house, she assured me that Andy and I could live with her for as long as we wanted.

Over and over again she reminded me, "If somebody, a stranger asks you where you're from…just point at my house and say over there. That's all they need to know."

For the first time in my life, I felt like I'd been accepted and not pre-judged. All the dreadful fear, that was stored in my body, floated away, with each passing day. Even Andy was happy and growing-up big and strong. I had become a part of a culture…a wonderful family. God carried me to a safe place and I was completely happy! More than ever, I became aware of nature that surrounded me. I was one with the land, the wind and all living creatures.

The spring brought new life, budding and singing, jumping, and playing. The summer's warmth covered me with rays of golden sunlight. Laughter and joy filled my eyes and ears, watching the children enjoy their first summer's swim. Fall brought the beauty of the rainbow of leaves and the reminder of the cycle of life, birth then death, covered by the pure white blanket of winter's first snow.

The Native Americans taught me many skills. I learned about teepees, how to make moccasins, belts, jewelry, and beading. I even danced native dances at POW WOWS. In turn, I gave them copies of my poems. They especially made a fuss over **FOOTPRINTS** and encouraged me to write more. Early one morning, encompassed by all of nature's beauty, I sat by a stream, pencil and paper in hand and created a special tribute to my friend Ruby, whose genuine love and kindness, remains in my heart, to this very day. The poem read:

IF YOU HAD WALKED IN MY MOCCASINS?

If you had walked in my moccasins, then you would know
The smell of rain before it rains,
The feel of cold before it snows
You would walk so proudly with your head held high
And enjoy the beauty of a summer sky.

If you had walked in my moccasins
You would fish from the sea
Gather food from the land and medicines from a tree
Wear meaningful feathers, and colorful beads
And become one with God for everyone of your needs

Sell jewelry, rugs, and tomahawks too
Arrows and trinkets, just to mention a few.
I have come a long way, through the trails of tears
Lived through poverty, sickness and overcome fears

I'm a true American...that I always will be
Do you think that I live in the land of the free?

Yet you wave the flag, the red, white and blue,

As you say to my people, maybe God will bless you?

In the darkest of night…In your silent of prayers

Have you thought of the sorrow our red brothers' bear?

If you had walked in my moccasins, then you would know

You too are my brothers…What you reap you shall sow

If you had walked in my moccasins, then you would know.

Then you would know.

Mary Stevenson

Ruby was washing clothes on an old wooden wash board, behind the house. Slowly I crept up behind her.

"Ruby I have a gift for you from Andy and me!" I shouted.

Startled, she turned around and held her chest. Her hands were dripping wet.

I felt uncomfortable trying to find the right words but continued, "You've taken good care of us and…given us a place to stay. We have no money but would be honored if you would accept this small token of our love."

Then I proudly presented her with my new poem. Quickly, she wiped her hands on her apron and accepted the poem.

As she read the words, giant tears poured down her face. I felt awkward. Never before had anyone seen Ruby cry. Only the sound of the wind could be heard in the moment of silence that encompassed us. Even Andy, who was playing with a wooden stick doll, halted his play and stare up at Ruby.

"This belongs to my people." Ruby's words broke the silence. "This is not for my eyes alone. These words echo the plight of God's proud people, yet whisper the hope for all mankind…I will share these with everyone." Ruby looked straight ahead, walked into the house and soon returned with the poem enclosed in a handmade, wood-carved frame.

"Thank you Mary Stevenson, Yellow Hair… no greater gift have I ever received." As Ruby smiled, the sun graced her golden-red face. I had never seen her look so radiant.

Away she walked, with the framed poem held close to her heart, toward the home of our Chief. I picked up Andy and held him feeling a great since of pride. God had truly given me a gift. By allowing His words to flow through me, troubled souls could be reached.

I kept in touch with my family back home, through letters. They did not approve of my living on an Indian reservation. On many occasions they had asked me to come home. But I wasn't budging. I would have stayed with my Native American family, the rest of my life, if it hadn't been for the war. On December 7th 1942, the Japanese bombed Pearl Harbor. I received word from my older sister Helen that our brother Andrew had been shipped off to war.

Months later, a letter came from my father, stating that Andrew was coming home on a short leave then he was to be shipped overseas. In this letter, I was also assured that Tony would most certainly be joining the soldiers overseas. Come home immediately, was inscribed at the end of the letter, and accompanied by a train ticket.

I had to see my brother. My mind traveled back to when we were kids and how we all stuck together. No one picked on one Stevenson without dealing with the entire gang. Andrew fought many of my battles for me. I remembered one evening being chased home from school by a bunch of older boys chanting "Tar Babies! They're so poor they eat tar from roofs!"

Even though their words were true, it hurt deeply hearing them flung at you. Andrew saved what little pride I had left, when he intercepted their scowls with a left hook that landed on the jaw of the biggest bully.
"What if something terrible would happen to him while he was overseas?" I dreadfully thought.

I was torn between two families. With great sadness, I told Ruby and the others that I had to go back to Pennsylvania. When that day arrived, stoned-faced Ruby, wearing a wonderful big smile handed me a going away present. I opened the brown paper wrapping and observed a long, hand-made, beaded, maroon colored skirt, along with matching beaded moccasins. Everyone from the village formed a circle of friendship and love around me. Everyone wore a big smile.

"This is not goodbye." I tearfully told them. "I'm coming back soon."

Ruby took me aside, "Mary, don't make promises that you can't keep!"
I broke down and cried big elephant tears as she hugged me. She knew in her heart that she would never see me again and she was right.

As I boarded the train, A heavy feeling came over me. I settle Andy in the seat beside me. "What has God got in store for us now, little one?" I pondered. Andy looked up at me as his big brown eyes began searching my face. I reach down, hugged him and expressed, "We don't have to worry. We've got each other. We'll always be a family.

Minister Mary Stevenson Zangare

6 DANCE WHITE CRACKER DANCE

At first everyone was happy to see the baby and me but then the same old prejudices cropped its ugly head. I wasn't good enough. Everyone knew that I was this single mother with a small baby, no education, and no job skills. To top it off, dad remarried and moved away, leaving Andy and me in an empty house. I promptly began looking for employment. It was difficult, with little education and literally no real job skills. But finally, I landed a job at a local coffee shop. I became skilled at making Submarine Sandwiches. Tony found out that I was back and began hanging around the coffee shop.

He acted like nothing had ever happened between us. I couldn't figure out why the service hadn't nabbed him. He immediately brought Andy gifts, which at first I didn't accept, then I softened-up. I felt that it was unfair to Andy not to be able to have the nicer things, because his mother was so poor. After all, Tony was his father. I even let Tony take Andy to visit his family. He always brought him back on time. In no time, I became comfortable with this arrangement.

One morning at work I felt a horrible pain in my side and lower back. My temperature shot up and perspiration soaked my uniform. My boss told me to go home, but I swore that it was nothing. You see I needed every dime to provide a living for Andy and me. I couldn't get sick! But the pain got so bad that I finally passed out, in the middle of the diner. When I awoke, I found myself in the hospital. My appendix had ruptured. Immediately, I asked the nurse about Andy. The nurse informed me that his father had taken him home.

A week later, as soon as I was released, from the hospital, I rushed to see Tony, who was living with his mother. I hurried up the steps to the familiar front door and knocked. There was no answer. I knew that Tony was home because his car was in the driveway and he allowed no one to drive <u>his</u> car. All of a sudden a thought jolted me. "What if he refuses to give Andy back?" I thought no...no and knocked on the door much harder and louder. Slowly the door crept opened. There stood Tony with pile of papers in his hand.

"Where's Andy? Is he all right?" I hysterically pleaded.
"Here these are for you," he scowled and shoved the papers in my outreaching hands.

"What are these Tony?" I questioned.

"Are you that stupid? Can't you read?" he pompously snapped. "They're divorce papers and I've got temporary custody of my son. You're not fit to be his mother. I don't even want him to ever see you again...ever!"
I felt the air from the door, as he slammed it in my face. I couldn't believe what had just occurred. I was handed divorce papers and told that I was unfit to even see my own son.

My heart and soul left me. If I hadn't had God's words to comfort me, I certainly would have jumped off the nearest bridge. I asked God over and over again to please help me, carry me guide me. I couldn't stand to lose my child to this evil cruel man, who robbed me of so much happiness and joy.

I cried and cried day and night. I became so depressed that I lost my job at the diner. I quit eating. Hunger pains from the past filled my stomach, but

I welcomed these pains, reasoning that God must be punishing me for leaving my husband.

By the time I appeared in court, I had lost so much weight that my bones were sticking out. The entire ordeal became a blur in my mind. The judge asked how much money that I had on me? I told him $10.00. Then he granted Tony and his mother custody of Andy until I had the means to support him. He concluded, then, I could return to his court, for another hearing. It wasn't what I had wanted to hear, but there was some ray of hope left. If I could find a job, then I could get my baby back.

First, I had to get away from Chester, where too many bad memories hovered over me. So I boarded a bus to Philadelphia. After wandering around, with pennies in my pocket, I noticed a sign that read, "**DANCERS WANTED**". I ran around back, to the stage door and banged on it as loudly as I could.

When the door finally opened, a short man with a big cigar in his mouth, and a Jersey accent announced that auditions were over. I pleaded with him to give me a chance. He must have felt sorry for me. I <u>was</u> a sight for sore eyes. My blond hair fell limp and lifeless on my shoulders and I weighed all of 90-lbs, soak and wet.

The man studied me then smiled and replied "Oh come on in and give it your best shot!"

There I stood center stage at the Troc Theater. One chandelier in that place probably cost more than my father's entire house.

"Hey Toots!"

I turned and saw the piano player glaring at me.

"Are you gonna just stand there?" he barked.

"No!" I yelled. "I'm gonna dance to **SWEET GEORGIA BROWN!** Can you play it?"

"Honey Lamb, I can play any song you can name!" he chuckled.

The music began and I danced. My entire body felt the rhythm. I was so light on my feet that I thought I could fly. Every fancy step, I had learned from my black brothers and sisters came back to me. In my mind I could hear all of them cheering me on saying, **"Dance WHITE CRACKER Dance! Dance WHITE CRACKER** Dance!" As the song ended, I concluded tap dancing with wings, with my feet flying two feet off of the floor. Scores of people began clapping.

The bright lights on the stage hid the fact that there were fifty people or more, consisting primarily of cast members seated in the audience. The show's director jumped onto the stage, shook my hand and declared "Honey Child you got the gig! What's your name?"

I thought for a second then blurted out "STEVEY RICHARDS!" By changing my name, I figured that I'd be safe from Tony and his mother. I wanted to pinch myself. I just landed a job at the Troc Burlesque Theater, as a dancer, making $50.00 a week.

After two weeks of rehearsal, the director discovered that I shined at doing impersonations of the stars including: Mae West (my favorite), Debbie Reynolds, Shirley Temple, Ella Fitzgerald, Kay Star and Kate Smith. I even played the spoons and tapped danced at the same time.

I loved every minute of being on stage. My down time was when the lights went out and I was alone in my apartment. But the blues did not last for long. God was carrying me and in my spare time, I carried my handwritten poems, His words to everyone! Although I terribly missed Andy, somehow I knew that God was carrying him too and that someday soon, we would be together.

I finally had a good paying job and was saving the money needed to win him back. Along with each new experience in my life, a brand new poem would pop into my head, like the poem that I dedicated to the chorus girls.

CHORUS GIRL

Once there was a Chorus Girl, all she could do was dance.

The town folk did not like her

And would not give her a chance.

She worked so hard every night,

Even danced before the Queen

Yet never spoke a displeasing word about the town so mean.

She danced here, there and everywhere

Paying every single bill

Finally she bought herself a house, high upon the hill.

When a flu epidemic struck the town,

Filling hospitals large and small

The town folk got together

And gave the mayor a desperate call.

They claimed they needed much more space

For hundreds who were ill

So they visited the chorus girl that lived upon the hill.

She met them with a heart-felt smile,

Then submitted to their plea

Her house is now a hospital that's called "Remember Me."

by Mary Stevenson

Mary's entire being seemed to be glowing. I was totally spellbound.

"Kathy, if I thought someone was down and out for the count, I would hand them a poem and say "You know, God was able to help me through my darkest hours and He most definitely will help you too! These are His words. I just push the pencil."

Mary sat there quietly. She seemed to be reflecting on a great thought and then she continued. "Out of all of the poems that I handed out, **FOOTPRINTS** was by far the most popular."

A perplexed look appeared on her face. She didn't understand why others were "awe struck" by, as she put it, her "little poem".

Mary, I interrupted. "God was able to touch millions of people, in some of the strangest places through **FOOTPRINTS**; people in jails, gutters, soup kitchens, truck stops, and who knows where else.

With a twinkle in her eye and a sly smile on her face she jokingly interjected; "Did I ever tell you the story about **FOOTPRINTS** saving a young dancer's life?"

I shook my head, smiled and answered; "Yes Mary…many, many times.

7 SECRETS

In August of 1979, Mary became a grandmother, again and at the end of the year, on the 9th of November, my daughter Karrie Marie Benoit was born. This was the day after Mary's birthday. I was in labor for 72 hours and finally, the baby was delivered c-section. When Mary received my good news, she laughed and conceded, "That kid wanted to celebrate her very own birthday! But…I'm so glad you had a little girl."

I was thoroughly busy being a new 1st time mom that it felt like the month of December sprouted wings and flew. Soon it was January 1980, a brand new year. Later that month, I received a call from Mary…except it didn't sound like her voice. In choppy, tear-filled sobs, she slowly formed words that uttered, "Basil just died."

I tried to console her but soon realized that her entire world had been torn apart. Basil was the only person who truly understood her and loved her unconditionally. Somehow we all got through the funeral. Weeks later, Mary still walked around in a dream-like stupor. She said that she couldn't help but think that Basil would come home and walk through the front door, at any moment! Every time she went to sleep, he was in her dreams.

I knew that it was time for one of our "let's get away and chat" sessions. Jim watched Karrie, while I picked up Mary. Our destination was the nearest Denny's for a long Saturday afternoon lunch. Once we were seated, neither one of us exchanged a word. I couldn't help but notice the dark circles and shadows underneath her eyes and how her hands shook as she attempted to steady the menu. After we placed our orders, I asked Mary if there was anything I could do to help her?

"Just love that new baby girl of yours...cause you never know in life what can happen."

The inquiring look on my face prompted Mary's next words.

"I've told very few people about this...but it hurts too much keeping too many secrets. Secrets can sometimes rob you of your life, you know...Do you want to hear a sad story...a secret?" she asked.

"If you want to tell me," I timidly replied.

Mary sipped her coffee then spoke from the depths of her heart. "For six months, I danced in Philly at the Troc, saved-up my money, in hopes to travel to Chester to get Andy back. Once a week, I'd send him cards and little gifts but they would all be returned. On the outside of the unopened package, in big red letters, were the words "return to sender". These people hated me. I knew that someday I would be in for quite a court battle.

Considering the Amalfitano's had the money and the clout and the fact that I had neither.

"It was show time!" The stage manager shouted. All week, I had rehearsed a new Hawaiian dance routine and was thrilled that I was getting the chance to shine in my own solo spotlight. Tonight was my night. I was Heddy Lamar, Mae West and Rita Haywood all wrapped-up into one. I felt like a famous movie star.

The room was filled to capacity. I heard the words "Stevey you're on" and hurried to center stage, dressed from head to toe in authentic Hawaiian hula attire. The twenty-piece band in the orchestra pit magically poured out the sounds of Hawaii, throughout the entire room. As the curtain rose, I felt the island rhythm overpower my senses and danced like never before. My moment was crudely interrupted by a familiar voice that could be heard shouting, over the music,

"That's no hula dancer! That's my ex-wife!"
Laughter filled the room. Totally humiliated I stopped dancing and ran off the stage to the dressing room. I flopped down in the nearest chair, in front of the mirror and cried like a baby. Dark mascara covered my face. "You see Mary," I scolded myself. "Just when you think things are going to work out, trouble rears its ugly head."

Tony bolted through the door, grabbed my arm and yelled; "You dumb slut! You'll never get Andy now, after I tell the judge that you've been dancing in a place like this. I should knock your...."
One of the male dancers grabbed Tony's closed fist; "If you want to fight someone Bub, why don't you tackle someone who'll give you a real go at it! Only cowards beat women!"

Tony rapidly withdrew his hand, looked around and found himself encircled by my fellow cast members. Quickly, he turned and ran for the door. The others laughed and taunted "Look at the big man run!"
I was again grateful for my new family of friends, God had surrounded me with. But I knew that Tony was right. This was the 1940's and people didn't respect chorus girls. Even though I never accepted a drink or a date, I was stilled viewed, in their eyes, as a fallen woman. The next day, I reluctantly quit my job as a dancer and returned to Chester. I rationalized

that I could at least be closer to my sisters and little Andy. Maybe I could peak at him through a fence or at the park.

I found a nice apartment and got my old job back at the coffee shop.

For a while it seemed like old times again, when I was a kid, before Tony. I went dancing every weekend never lacking dates. Men seemed to flock all around me. One day my older sister Muriel, who was married to a wonderful, successful man named Joe, asked me to come over to her house for lunch. This was a rare request. Although we got along, we normally didn't socialize. We would only get together during infrequent family occasions (like funerals) and sometimes during the holidays. Out of curiosity, I accepted her invitation.

Muriel's home was decorated very nicely with all the trimmings that I someday wished to possess. I sat on the sofa beside her that looked completely brand new. All of a sudden, I noticed some furniture that had once belonged to our mother.

I thought, "How come I was never given any of these furnishings, especially when my son and I lived in that empty house."

"Mary," Muriel broke the ice. "Joe and I have been talking and we have some advice for you."

The way she looked at me made me feel very uncomfortable like a bad kid in the principal's office.

"The entire town is talking about how you're flaunting yourself on every single man in town. Some of the wives of the <u>married</u> men are even complaining about your behavior."

I was outraged. "Muriel, I've done nothing wrong. I can't help it if men find me attractive!" I boldly defended.

"Well, the only reason they hang all over you is because you are a <u>divorcee</u>." She taunted.

I thought, "What was wrong with being divorced? Everyone in town was aware of my circumstances with Tony. There were no secrets in a town that size. I couldn't figure out why they were condemning me? Were they also condemning Tony? He was a divorcee too!"

I stood up and headed for the door and shouted, "If you choose to think badly of me, then who am I to stop you!" Then I slammed the door behind me. My thoughts rang louder and louder as I walked down the street; "Who does she think she is? She found a good husband. She's the lucky one. Joe will do anything for her. I'm going to ignore her and the whole damned town."

That weekend, I went to the dance hall as usual but this time I didn't feel like dancing. All I could think about was Muriel's unfair words. "Was Muriel telling me the truth? No…it was silly to think that men could be that dishonest and shallow. Maybe she was jealous of my being so free and unattached." I began to mentally scrutinize every man that walked up and asked me to dance. After turning down about a dozen of their offers, I decided that I had had enough and was ready to walk, unescorted, back to my apartment. Normally I had numerous offers from gentlemen, begging to give me a ride home, but tonight I was mad at the world. The madder I got the faster I walked.

"What if men <u>do</u> look at me as an object, a plaything, a <u>divorcee</u>? I'll show them. I don't need any of them." I muttered out loud. Then suddenly, I felt a great weight brutally press down on my shoulders. I quickly turned and saw a tall, dark disheveled looking man, breathing down on me.

"You <u>know</u> what I want baby." The words slurred out of his mouth, filling the air with a foul smell of alcohol.

The next thing that I knew, I was lying in the wet bushes with my clothes torn into shreds. A savage unclean beast had violated me. I had been raped. I felt so ashamed. Slowly, I gathered my things and secretly headed for home. New, horrible thoughts screamed loudly in my head, "No one will believe you. They'll all say that the town floozy probably got what she deserved." Finally I made it home. Immediately I filled the tub with hot water, and tried to scrub myself clean. It did not matter how hard I scrubbed, I could not get clean.

The next weeks were nightmarish. I wasn't able to remember people's orders. I lived in fear thinking that at anytime that monster would enter the coffeehouse and further violate me…or even worse…tell the world that he raped me…therefore exposing <u>my</u> shame.

A month later I began feeling sick. Oh my God…I was pregnant. I feared that Tony and his mother would soon find out and announce the news, all over town. "That child doesn't belong to our family." What would little

Andy think? A friend of mine suggested that I get a back street abortion. I shuddered at the thought. Alone in my apartment, I turned to God and pleaded, "Please help me! You promised me if I believed in you, that you would never leave me or forsake me. Where are you now, when I need you the most?" I cried and cried a mountain of tears.

Just then Muriel burst through the door. My wails could be heard out in the street. "Mary what on earth is wrong?" she asked as she grabbed tissues from her purse and shoved them in front of my swollen face.

Desperately I tried to shut off my teary faucet. I grabbed more tissues, wiped my eyes, but still couldn't control my muffled sobs.

"I came over to apologize for not defending your honor." Muriel happily announced.

I cried and wailed even harder and more uncontrollably. Then, she sat down beside me and held me in her arms, like I was a baby. "Stevey, there's something dreadfully wrong here. Tell me what it is so that I can help you." I poured my heart out to her not skipping a single detail. After I had finished, she carefully commented that she wanted to discuss my plight with Joe.

I straightened up and frantically yelled, "No! I don't want anyone else to know what had happened. First of all nobody will believe me and it would kill daddy."

Muriel gently took my hand and explained, "Mary this is a blessing in disguise. Joe and I have always wanted children, from the day we first said I do… but we weren't able." Tears filled her eyes. "Please let me to talk to

Joe about raising this baby as our own. Think about it. How are you going to raise a child, being a single mother? You've already tried that and look where it got you. You're lucky that Andy didn't wind up in an orphanage adopted-out to strangers. You would be doing something great for the baby, yourself, and Joe and me. Think long and hard about it." She kissed my forehead, turned and walked out the door.

I thought about it, long and hard. "My life was a mess. They had everything a baby could ever want and need. This would be best for the baby." I heard my inner voice say…"Okay."

I continued to work in the coffee shop until I was seven months pregnant. It was too difficult to try and hide my condition, so I had to quit my job. During the rest of my pregnancy, Muriel and Joe helped me with the food and rent. Then that joyful and painful day came, the day my little girl was born. I felt like both heaven and earth had crushed in on me. Here she was in my arms so tiny so pretty and new. Soon I had to give her away and forever become Aunt Mary.

The birth had not been an easy one. Complications developed. I was told that I must immediately have an operation. Since my hospital stay would have to be extended, Muriel and Joe took the baby that I called "Babe" to their home…until I recuperated. Then they promised that they would return her to me, temporarily.

After the operation, the doctor entered my room and spoke in a matter-of-fact, cold tone, "Mary, the operation was successful but the problem was more serious then we had originally thought. You were full of infection and therefore we had no other option but to perform a complete hysterectomy.

"Oh my God! What have you done." I cried out. "I can't have any more children!"

I wished that I had died. After my release from the hospital, my life became as empty as my apartment. Muriel no longer visited. Furthermore she suggested that I wait some weeks before coming to see Babe, so that they could bond with their new child. I was completely alone and devastated. I knew that God had abandoned me and thought, maybe He was paying me back, for being such an unruly child, a bad daughter, an unfit mother, and a lousy wife. According to the minister, at my mother's funeral, God was the culprit who even took my mother away from me! But this was the ultimate betrayal.

It was God's fault that I was even born. I read my copy of **FOOTPRINTS**, crumpled it up, and threw it on the floor. Then I walked into the kitchen, turned on the gas stove and placed my head into the oven. Everything instantly blacked out like someone switched off a light.
Throb, throb, throb, my head was pounding. My stomach was nauseous. I was feeling horrible from head to toe.

Was I dead? Was I in hell? I had to find out. Slowly I opened my eyes and found myself in a total white room. My arms wouldn't move. It seemed they had been strapped down to the bed. A crumpled-up piece of paper was lying on my bed stand. Then all of a sudden, the paper sprang up and danced in midair. The words left the paper and read themselves out loud to me, "One night I dreamed I was walking along the beach with the Lord. Many scenes of my life flashed across the sky"...it was **FOOTPRINTS.** Frantically, I woke up from that horrible nightmarish hell. Although I discovered that my arms were strapped down, I was relieved knowing that my mind was still intact. Then I looked at the table beside my bed. I couldn't believe my eyes. There was my crumpled-up copy of **FOOTPRINTS.** Someone had brought it to me.

"Father forgive me for I have sinned!" I chanted over and over again. . I turned my eyes to heaven and made the most sacred vows... "I never again would blame God for my choices. Never again would I attempt to take away the precious life that He had given me. I counted and I had a purpose in life. I was put on earth to help others...not to feel sorry for myself and not to commit...I shuddered to even think of the word. God carried me again."

Mary sat silently sipping her coffee. I felt so sorry for Mary, not knowing what to say. The air became so heavy in the restaurant that I had to somehow change the subject.

"How did you and Basil meet? Oh"...I had not intended to bring up the subject of Basil. Without any thought, the words escaped my mouth. I felt like an idiot. A pregnant pause followed. Mary saw that I was uncomfortable with the subject.

"I don't mind talking about Basil. He was the true love of my life." She courageously announced as she continued.

"I had gathered enough money and courage to take Tony back to court. Tony was wearing a new suite and his mother, an expensive fur. Even their attorney was better dressed than my attorney. The judge quickly heard the case and just as quickly sided with Tony. He concluded that Andy lived in a most suitable home and in a stable environment. This was also how Tony managed to stay out of the service. He claimed that he was a single parent raising his son all alone.

However the judge gave me visiting privileges. Once every two weeks, I could take my son for an outing in the afternoon. It wasn't what I wanted to hear but it was better than nothing at all.

What judges say and what actually happens are two different things. When I would show up to take Andy for our outing, he would rarely be there. Sometimes I was lucky to see him for ten minutes and that was only because I would show up early and unannounced.

I had no money to take Tony back to court. It was also difficult being Aunt Mary to my little girl, Babe. Then my oldest sister Helen and her husband Bob, who had moved and settled in Southern California, invited me to live with them until I found my own place. I had always loved movie stars. George Raft was my favorite actor. As a kid, I got myself into more trouble, staying out late, watching George Raft movies. I thought, who knows, I might be able to run right into him. It was common knowledge that the streets of Hollywood were always full of famous stars. So I gladly took them up on it.

Once I arrived in California, I loved it especially the warm sun, the ocean, and oranges dangling from trees. When I was a kid, I thought that oranges only came out at Christmas time. I was in paradise. In no time, I got a job as nurses' aide. Every weekday, I rode the bus to and from work. During the long ride home, I would often fall asleep and miss my stop. On this one particular evening, I was bound and determined to get off the bus at my designated stop. Intensely, I focused on the bus door. When the bus stopped, I barreled through the other passengers, out the door, taking another male passenger out of the door with me. His name was Basil Zangare.

It was love at first sight. From that moment on we did everything together, dancing, sightseeing, going to the movies, bowling. It wasn't long before he asked me to marry him. Without any hesitation, I accepted. Even my sister Helen, after putting him through a thorough interrogation, liked Basil. We worked together as a team. I told him all of my secrets and he understood and confessed that he loved me even more.

He wanted children, but, as you know, I wasn't able. So we adopted a child and spoiled the heck out of him...he was so cute, fat and cuddly."
Mary's eyes watered, "I've been through some oppressing, disastrous, times, but losing the one you love, is far worse.
There was a feeling of relief that came over both of us, when the waitress arrived with our food.
"Let me say the blessing," I insisted.

Mary nodded in agreement. "God bless Mary in her time of need. Comfort her. Help her realize that Basil is in a better place free from sorrow and pain and that someday they will reunite. Amen."

Mary smiled and repeated "Amen!"

By the time I dropped Mary off in front of her house the sun was already beginning to set. "Wait here," she requested as she jumped out of the car and ran for the house.

I watched her 200-pound-plus body, gracefully, run up the stairs and thought, "For a heavy-set lady, in her late fifties, she sure gets around pretty good." As quickly as she scampered off, she was back again with a piece of paper in her hand. As I rolled down the window, she handed me the paper. In a panting, breathy tone she said, "Read this!"

OH LITTLE GIRL OF MINE

Oh little girl of mine when I am old and gray
Will you someday remember me or have me put away?
Will you call me up to chat
About your happiness or strife?
Or let me hold you in my arms, I've waited all my life.

My face may be wrinkled; I may not walk strait and tall
Can you make sure I have glasses
So I can see you when you call?
I leave you my family Bible,
Oh yes of course my beads of pearl
My daddy gave them to me when I was a little girl.
Although you owe me nothing, oh how happy I would be
To see your face once in a while
Oh please remember me.

Mary Stevenson

I looked at Mary with wide eyes, fighting back tears of emotion. "Can I keep this?" I quietly asked.

"Sure," Mary replied. "I've got plenty more where those came from!"
She hugged me through the window then I drove away. During the drive home, I kept reflecting on her words and thought, "She does have an abundance of poems... a wealth of words... God's given her words to share with anyone who will just take the time to read... The world needs to know about Mary Stevenson. Her work has remained a secret for too long."

New recording tells tale of beaten child

Mary & Kathy collaborating in order to fight Child Abuse by releasing a new recording called "Momma Don't You Love Me"

8 WHAT IS THE COLOR OF LOVE?

Karrie was rapidly growing and soon crawling all over the small two-bedroom apartment. I felt that it was time for me to go back to work at the country club. Two months later, Mary was crying on the phone again. "Mary what's wrong?" I inquired.

She constantly was bouncing from grieving over Basil, repairing her home, to putting out fires with her kids. In my heart, I knew that she had to soon snap out of it. I advised her to sell her house and move closer to Hollywood, that way she could audition for roles in movies. Her brother-in-law, Joe suggested that she sell the house and move to Las Vegas. She took his advice.

When Mary chose Las Vegas, it didn't completely surprise me. Since the day we played The Sahara, she vowed that she would dwell in the land of showgirls, bright lights and slot machines. She reasoned that if she permanently lived in Las Vegas, then she could easily find an agent, get weekend bookings and do stand-up comedy.

With the proceeds from the sale of the house, Mary gave her son a substantial amount of money; purchased some new clothes, then put the rest in the bank. Her interest check combined with her Social Security benefits afforded Mary, for the first time in her life, financial stability.

Her apartment complex was for adults only. She lived in a freshly painted spacious two-bedroom, apartment covered with thick plush carpeting. It resembled a little dollhouse, complete with all brand new furniture. Every wall was lined with pictures and plaques, the same that were found in her California home. She was thrilled showing off the place as well as the pool, recreational-room and other facilities. Right next door, in walking distance, stood the Continental Casino, where Mary played slots and bingo.

The majority of her time was spent swimming, gambling and socializing, with her newfound friends whose backgrounds ranged from dancers, comediennes, singers, to street people. She even joined some of them on a Hawaiian cruise.

Once a month I would visit. A few years had passed and during one visit, I noticed that Mary was feeling terribly down. She said she loved Vegas but felt that her efforts to promote **FOOTPRINTS** and her other poetry had come to a complete halt. In gift stores, all over the Vegas Strip, she discovered hundreds of copies of **FOOTPRINTS** signed, Author Unknown or "Anonymous". When she would mention to her friends that she was the author, they would scoff at her and accuse her of being a liar. I suggested that she apply for a copyright on her Footprints poem, then at last she could show others that she was the true author. She loved the idea and went right to work, mailing in her form in to the U.S. Government's Library of Congress, Copyright Office. A couple of months later, Mary called screaming over the phone.

"I got it! I got it!"

"You got what?" I asked.

"I got my copyright on **FOOTPRINTS!** Now everyone will know for sure that I am the author. Now they'll stop calling me a liar. Thank you Kathy, You don't know what this means to me and thank you God, for sending me good friends!"

It felt good knowing that I was able to do something to help someone whose words had aided so many people. But it also saddened me knowing the pain, that Mary was going through, by constantly being accused of lying, whenever the subject of **FOOTPRINTS** came-up…what a two edged sword.

On another occasion, Mary and I discussed forming an organization to help prevent child abuse. Every day in the newspaper, we would read articles about beaten and starved children. Mary's poem **THE LITTLE SEED** echoed the abused child's plea for help. I took the poem off of her wall, held it in my hands and began to meditate, informing Mary that I would have a song by morning. In the middle of the night a sad melody entered in my head, then the words from her poem mingled with mine and messed with the melody. I jumped up, flipped on a light and found a piece of paper and a pencil (Two items always available at Mary's). Then I copied down the new words and notes to guide the melody. The next morning I presented Mary with the song:

MOMMA DON'T YOU LOVE ME?

I am from a little seed grown to a tiny child

Reaching out to those round me for comfort and a smile.

Everything was doin' fine until one day I cried

I got beat so badly and I had nowhere to hide

Chorus:

Momma don't you love me? Am I oh so bad?

You're all I have in life the good times and the sad.

I stopped crying scared with fright.

What could the matter be?

I couldn't sleep, I couldn't eat, Oh why do they hurt me?

Chorus: Momma don't you love me? Am I oh so bad?
You're all I have in life the good times and the sad.

Some people say that we don't know because we are so small.
Pain is not a way of life. LOVE will conquer all.

Chorus: Momma you can love me. I am not so bad.
You're all I have in life the good times and the sad.
You're all I have in life the good times and the sad.

With tears rolling down her cheeks Mary cried out, "I love it! It's beautiful and I can't believe you captured the meaning of the poem…exactly!"
I gave Mary a puzzled look.

She continued, "When I was a nurse's aide, right after Basil and I got married, I was working in the emergency room, when a battered little girl was wheeled by me. Her little face was swollen, black and blue. Without thinking, I ran over to the stretcher and grabbed her tiny hand. Her mother wasn't far behind ran and grabbed her other limp hand. The child opened her eyes, stared at her mother and painfully uttered, "Mama if I die, then will you love me?"

"I found out later, that evening that the little girl passed away. Her mother had beaten her to death. Her words continue to haunt me to this day. That's why I wrote **THE LITTLE SEED**. Your spirit guided you to a higher understanding when you captured the true meaning hidden in the poem."

I had no words to say. This confirmed what I was already feeling, that we had to go forward with our new assignment. No doubt this had been a divine sign.

"We've got to get it out to all the radio stations." Mary passionately announced.

I laughed and added, "First we have to get a decent recording of it made."
I went back to Los Angeles and began to assemble the necessary musicians. Three years prior, I had hired mostly the same musicians and completed my first album **KATHY BEE STINGS.** We were planning on touring, promoting the album, but funds became short. Jim, Karrie and I returned to Southern California and Jim and I picked up day gigs. Jim worked for a photo copier company and I managed apartment buildings during the day and sang in a duo act, on evenings and weekends. Our personal relationship, in my eyes, had always been rocky, but after we returned from our whirlwind tour, things were starting to get worse.

My life took another spin. I was pregnant, again. On August 11,1984, at the same time of 1984 Olympics was held in Las Angeles (In which Jim and I had tickets to the final diving event), I went into labor, seven weeks early. On that very day a 5-pound 3-ounce baby boy, named James Weston Roy Benoit was delivered… prematurely?

Six months later, our Anti-Child Abuse songs were completed. The A-side was **MOMMA DON'T YOU LOVE ME** and on the B-side was the song **GROWNING UP ALONE** written by Kathleen Parente` and myself. Liz owner of **Erika Records** pressed the single, on her label. Mary and I mailed out hundreds of records, to radio stations, across the country.

We included response cards. The majority of the responses came back favorable. We were elated… The public liked our song.

For three years straight, the song **MOMMA DON'T YOU LOVE ME** picked up numerous local and state awards. Members of the California Country Music Association voted it "Best Song of the Year" and "Best Record of the Year". I also received awards for being "Best Entertainer" and "Female Vocalist of the Year".

Mary and I researched and visited Child Abuse Centers then donated proceeds from concert. At the concerts, we passed out Child Abuse literature. During this time, many reporters interviewed us and Mary was able to declare to them that she wrote **Footprints In The Sand.** What a joyous time it was for Mary when she finally read the words, in her local newspaper; **Footprints In The Sand** by *Mary Stevenson*. More than ever, she was delighted sharing her poems with her new fans.

Although people were impressed, by Mary's story, no one offered her any solution regarding reclaiming **FOOTPRINTS**…or publishing **WHITE CRACKER.**

One of our Child Abuse Concerts took place in Las Vegas, in the parking lot of Mary's apartment building. A variety of performers joined in and donated their time and talent. Mary was the comedienne/MC and I sang. All together, we raised $2,000.00. It felt great showing that we cared enough and were willing to try and make a difference.

Later on that evening, when everyone left, Mary and I were sitting around her apartment going over our next show. I asked her if she had ever been involved in a project like this, where she helped raise money for others?

"Oh sure," she laughed. "I'm a Viet-Mom."

I gave her puzzled look and asked, "Okay, I've heard of Vietnam my brother was there. But what's a Viet-Mom?"

"Wait here, I'll be right back." She announced and headed for her bedroom. Momentarily, she returned with an armful of scrapbooks and a box of pictures and laid them in my lap, as she sat down beside me.

A peculiar feeling came over me. "Mary, my only brother, Marion served in Vietnam and was wounded."

"Oh, I'm sorry." She said with a sorrowful look on her face.

"He made it back home...but later died in a car crash in 1975, a month later... Jim and I decided to get married." I soberly replied.

As I went through the numerous pictures, newspaper clippings and letters, Mary told me her story.

"In the 1960's while the world was watching the war in Vietnam on their televisions, I was thinking about what I could do to help those poor boys fighting over there."

"Was your son in Vietnam?" I asked.

"No," Mary replied. Not personally…but I felt that it was my calling to do something. At that time I had become an ordained minister, primarily I taught children. Then this idea came to mind. The first person, I informed about my idea was Basil. I announced, honey. I'm going to bake Christmas cookies for our soldiers in Vietnam.

He answered, "You're gonna do what? By the way, it's not Christmas… it's October. Soon it will be Halloween?

Basil knew that when I put my mind to it, then that's exactly what I was going to do! After the initial shock wore off, he loving gave me the support that I needed. That's one of the things that I loved about him. He always let me do what I felt I had to do. Then, I contacted the Girl Scouts, Boy Scouts, Churches and community sponsored groups and told them that my kitchen would be open, round the clock. I put ads in the local paper. The local grocery stores donated sugar, butter, eggs and flour.

Other companies donated boxes. Movie theaters gave us day old popcorn to pack the cookies and other goodies in. In some boxes I packed poems, sometimes Bibles, hand knitted items and chewing gum. **FOOTPRINTS** proved to be the most appropriate one to send. It's hard to imagine being that far away from your home, family and country. I wanted them to know that God was everywhere and that He would carry them through.

People came from "out of the word-work" to help in the kitchen. Basil's garage was totally taken over with boxes and dry goods. He would smile and say, "I'll be glad to see Christmas, so that things can get back to normal around here and I can finally park my car in my garage."

Mary eagerly ran over to the wall and removed a small frame, then held it in front of my eyes and asked, "Do you see the pass enclosed in this frame?" I shook my head yes, feeling overwhelmed by Mary and all the materials surrounding me.

"This is the plaque that was given to me by the Vietnamese enemy forces. I can travel in enemy territory at anytime with this pass."

I waited for her to answer the "why" look on my face.

Mary continued. "After the boys received their packages, they wrote back stating other items that they needed; little things like toothpaste, catsup, candy to larger items like books and used clothing for the poor and abandoned Vietnamese children. So I hopped right to it and sent as many items as I could get my hands on. The Vietnamese forces were so grateful they sent me this pass! My oven was on from October the 15th until December the 15th. We sent over 7,000 schoolbooks, blankets, and clothes to the Vietnamese children. One snap shot, sent to me by a soldier, showed a child in my son's old tee shirt. This made me feel good! But baking cookies was our #1 goal."

"Mary you're like Bob Hope. So many young men were uplifted by your generosity and caring, at a most crucial time!" I added.
Then Mary urged me to read some of the soldier's letters. Each letter expressed so much gratitude and appreciation, for the warmth and caring that Mary and her friends had provided. It was hard for me to imagine, being a soldier, far away from home and given the job to fight, kill or be killed. What inner turmoil and moral pain, they must have experienced. One soldier's letter read:

"Mary I'm nineteen and very lonely. I look forward to your packages but mostly your letters. I don't know what I would do if you too would quit writing me. You see my own family stopped writing months ago."

That letter brought tears to my eyes. Mary had done so much, and with such little resources. Most of her life, she had been essentially poor, struggling just to live. Yet she always considered the needs of so many others.

"You see this here!" Mary proudly pointed to an old clipping, where the headlines read: **MARY ZANGARE BUENA PARKS WOMAN OF THE YEAR.**

"I was the guest of honor in a parade sponsored by The Walt Disney Company. Thank you cards poured in from everyone, even John Wayne, Edward G. Robinson, and Richard Nixon. But the most special of them all was the letter that I received from the President of the United States, Lyndon B. Johnson. He congratulated me on doing a great job and even signed the letter himself!"

Again, I didn't know what to say. After a period of silence went by, and Mary put her treasures away, I asked, "What poem did you write about The

Vietnam War, Mary?"

"I didn't write a poem about Vietnam." She solemnly replied.

I was really surprised. "Here's a lady who writes about every event in her life. Yet she didn't write about the war."

She must have been reading my thoughts because she added, "I was too busy answering hundreds of soldier's letters. But I did write a song."

In her scratchy voice she sang to me:

WHAT IS THE COLOR OF LOVE, LOVE, LOVE
IT COMES FROM HEAVEN ABOVE
WITH PEOPLE EVERYWHERE, THIS WORLD WE CAN SHARE
WHAT IS THE COLOR OF LOVE?

LET'S GET WORD AROUND, AROUND
THAT VICTORY CAN BE FOUND
IT COMES FROM ABOVE AS PURE AS A DOVE
WHAT IS THE COLOR OF LOVE?

WHEN THERE'S GREED, HATE AND SORROW
THEN WHAT'S LEFT FOR TOMORROW
THERE'S NOTHING TO GAIN
IF APART WE REMAIN

SO WHAT IS THE COLOR OF LOVE, LOVE, LOVE
IT COMES FROM GOD UP ABOVE
THERE'S ROOM FOR ONE ANOTHER
SHAKE HANDS WITH YOUR BROTHER
WHAT IS THE COLOR OF LOVE?

Mary Stevenson Zangare

I stood up and applauded her. "Mary, I'm surprised that I didn't see you on TV in one of those 1960's Anti-War protest marches!"

"There's more than one way to get your point across." She smiled and replied. "Those kids did what they had to do and I had to follow my own path."

Mary always seemed to march to a different drummer and listen to a different tune...and what a sweet tune she must have heard, as her footsteps followed His.

Mary Stevenson Zangare Getting records ready for airplay.

9 DEVOURING DIVORCE

1985 was not a good year for me. Jim and I were having escalating marital problems. We had always been "the opposites who attracted each other". Now, we were "the opposites who repelled". Our life together was becoming unbearable for me. I felt like we merely were going through the motions.

In the middle of the year, I decided to make a change and devote more time to my music career. So I quit my day job managing the apartments and continued to sing at night. Simultaneously, the record **MOMMA DON'T YOU LOVE ME** was receiving radio airplay along with some newspaper publicity. Unfortunately, the news of my success attracted a very unsavory character named James Black, who declared that he could launch my career, just like Colonel Tom Parker did with Elvis.

His credentials and references looked appropriate and everyone said that I needed a good manager. So I agreed to see what he could do. After months of false promises, wasted time and money, and after discovering that James had a big cocaine habit, I gave James the boot. However, I was left with large debts. The entire ordeal was completely devastating. I felt like a "lone" wiped-out warrior.

Mary was always there for me, whether it was to talk or just listen. Sensing, that I needed her, she visited more often and stayed longer than usual. We would make plans for future projects, as well as create new ideas, for old ones. Our Child Abuse Concerts were still in full swing but my personal life was in a shambles. I loved my two kids dearly but knew, in my heart, that Jim and I were not going to last. This fact, I could not keep from Mary. Many hours, she spent consoling and encouraging me.

"Say your prayers." She often reminded me. "God has a special plan for each and every one of us."

In the meantime, I had to get some steady work, so I formed a company called **P. R Productions**, wrote and published songs and sold records. Back in Las Vegas, Mary became involved in, The Ms. Senior Las Vegas contest, a beauty/talent contest for women over sixty. For months, she worked developing a new act, where she portrayed a grubby looking, bag lady, pushing a shopping cart, full of common human necessities. During a five-minute joke routine, she displayed items, of toilet paper, plastic bags, jars, strings and cans. Next she tap-danced to **SWEET GEORGIA BROWN** and played the spoons. For her grand finale, in full hobo attire, with a painful, sorrowful look on her face, she recited her deeply moving poem, "Homeless Hungry Tired And Cold".

HOMELESS HUNGRY TIRED AND COLD

Lord what is this all about?

Why am I doing without?

I'm homeless, hungry, tired and cold.

I come to you without pity.

I live here in the "Silver City"

Yet I'm homeless, hungry, tired and cold.

My home it burnt down to the ground.

Nothing but misery, I have found.

My eyesight is now failing me.

I call on You to help me see.

No longer can I go on this way.

No longer do I wish to stay.

I'm homeless, hungry, tired and cold.

Your story I've been often told,

Of how You love both young and old.

Just take me by my feeble hand

And lead me to Your Promise Land.

Please let me stay there by Your side.

I know that I'd be satisfied.

Please, forgive me for my words so bold.

Lord, I'm homeless, hungry, tired and cold.

Mary Zangare

The audience roared with delight. Mary again completely captivated her subjects. Although she took second place runner-up as Ms. Senior Las Vegas, she won the talent portion by unanimous vote.

By the time 1986 roared in, Jim and I were at total odds. It was difficult, trying to overcome the damage from my coke head manager, who left me in debt, during the Christmas Season. Coupled with putting together a new company, taking care of two kids and trying to keep the bills paid, required many sleepless, working hours. The other cloud that hung over my head was the fear that Jim would lose his job. In the past, Jim had been known to quit a job, at the drop of a hat and stay unemployed, for months. I was constantly on pins and needles wondering if I could keep my kids, housed and fed.

While temporarily working for Liz at Erika Records, a man walked in, who changed my life. He was the former Drag Racer, Don Hampton. We briefly talked, mostly about records. (He had sponsored a record that was shaped like a dragster.) The following day, He called Liz and wanted to know everything about me. Liz, being a close friend, was aware of my unhappy relationship. She too was having problems in her own marriage. Don and Liz proceeded to set up a dinner meeting with Chuck, (A man whom Liz adored and later married) and myself. The four of us met at a local restaurant. Instantaneously Don and I hit it off. In no time we poured our hearts out to each other. It seemed that we both were in unhappy, miserable, situations. Then out of the blue Don announced that he loved me and wanted to take care of me, for the rest of my life. I cried tears of joy. I felt as though I had been taking care of everyone else, for many years.

The most difficult thing for me to do was to tell my six-year-old daughter and my Ohio family, especially my mom and dad that I was leaving Jim and moving in with Don. This was totally against what I believed in… But I had asked Jim to move in with his relatives who lived in Orange County but he refused.

After the move, inwardly I felt as if heavy chains had been lifted from my heart, soul and life. My family and friends were shocked and expressed their dismay. This was a time when I had to make a change and it was difficult. Without Don's great strength and love, my younger sister Louvicia's words of kindness and support, along with the support of other close friends, I don't know how I could have survived this totally depressing ordeal.

Mary was always there for me. First hand, she witnessed the years of struggling and unhappiness that Jim and I were going through.

"Two people aren't always meant to be together," she said. Then she reminded me to read **FOOTPRINTS** and **AND YOU CARRIED ME.** "Remember, the Lord will keep you safe and guide you. "Unequally yoked people, don't always survive marriages." She added. During that time, she sent me a very strange poem:

DEVOURING DIVORCE

Devouring divorce, devouring yes.

It eats up your energy when you're depressed

If you've felt the sorrow, then this poem was written

For you, who've experienced pain and were smitten

When we were teenagers young and in love,

We sought no help from God above

On the day that we, had marriage in mind

We were joined together, yet were two of a kind.

We knew it all. We walked step by step,

Until the bills, one by one slowly crept.

Our financial woes had just begun

When our baby arrived out went the fun.

During life's routines, somehow something was missing

No more intimate talks, no more hugging and kissing

Did we grow up too fast? Find a separate course?

Now we both are faced with a devouring divorce.

By Mary Stevenson

I thought, "How could one person capture so many of our human sorrows and woes? She felt the pain of others; walked their walk and wasn't judgmental. Mary always offered help and comforted those in need. Like a doctor who prescribed medicine for sickness, Mary supplied remedies for the soul... her poetry."

The kids and I settled in at Don's and I immediately filed for a divorce. Don was the love of my life. He worked hard, six days a week, as the owner/operator of **HAMPTON BLOWERS**, where he sold superchargers to car, boat owners and drag racers. Yet he took the time to give special care and to support my two kids and me. He even changed 18-month-old Weston's diapers.

I told him all about Mary and was anxious for them to meet. One weekend, when the kids were with Jim, Don and I went to Vegas. Mary always put on the coffeepot, when she knew she was having company. She greeted us both with a warm, friendly smile and a bear hug. Oddly, I was seated on the coach, surrounded by "new" poems that she insisted that I read, while she led Don to the kitchen table, where they conversed. About twenty minutes later, while Don went to the restroom, Mary ran to me and whispered.

"I really like him Kathy. And he sure does love you and the kids. You've got a good one there. Don't let him slip away." She paused for a moment and looked toward the restroom, then softly continued, "Don reminds me of my Basil."

The restroom door flung open and Don walked out, smiling confidently as he strutted back into the kitchen, like he <u>knew</u> that he was the object of our conversation.

Mary giggled "See, I can tell by the way he looks at you, that he <u>really</u> does love you."

"And I love him too Mary," I replied.

"He'll be good to you, like Basil was good to me." She continued. "One summer, my sisters were all planning to take a trip to Hawaii. Robert Louis Stevenson is buried there, you know." She proudly announced. "I wanted to go so badly but realized that money was exceptionally tight. Basil secretly worked a second job, so I could go on the trip! Don is like Basil. He wants to make you happy."

Mary rejoined Don in the kitchen. I sat alone thinking, "I'm really happy that the two of them are getting along. He's Mr. Practical, she's Ms. Presumptuous ...definitely opposites...but I love them both."

At the end of the year, Don and I got married. We rented a paddleboat (neither one of us could swim) and the ceremony was held far away from land in the Pacific Ocean. Karrie was the flower girl; Weston, the ring bearer; my sister Louvicia, the bridesmaid; my dad gave me away, while my mom proudly watched. After we said our vowels, "Until the death of love, do we part," the air filled with cheers, from a boat full of our closest friends. It was a perfect day!

Mary had a ball. She owned the dance floor. All by herself, she tapped and put on quite a floorshow. Earlier that day, Mary handed me an old fashion bonnet and asked if I needed something old to wear during the ceremony? "Not today Mary, I have a veil," I cordially, but sternly replied.

After the ceremony, I noticed that she was talking to other guests...still holding that bonnet in her hand. After we docked and the wedding party climbed into the limousine, I made the comment "I wonder what idiot Mary got to wear her stupid bonnet?"

An enormous grin covered my father's face. I received my answer. Dad didn't have to say a word. Weeks later, Mary sent me the evidence...pictures of the wedding. There stood my father top deck wearing an old fashioned flowery ladies bonnet. From that moment on, Mary referred to my father, Harry Woodfork, as Chief War Bonnet.

Harry Woodfork Chief War Bonnet   Don & Kathy Bee Hampton

10 ENTERTAINERS AGAINST CHILD ABUSE

Although we talked on the phone at least twice a week, Mary didn't visit as often as she had when I was with Jim. I got the feeling that she was trying to give me some time alone, with my new husband. A couple of months later, I persuaded her to stay the weekend. During that visit, I asked how her book **WHITE CRACKER** was coming along? She commented that she was still waiting on Jackie, who now lived in Hollywood, to get a buyer for it. She planned on discussing the book with Jackie at the wedding, but became sidetracked.

"In that case, let's go visit her." I suggested.

Mary giggled and shook her head in agreement. After dialing Jackie's number and getting the green light, we hopped in my car and drove a half-hour away, to Hollywood. Jackie lived in a simple, little three-bedroom house, with an unattached garage in the back, in a very quiet neighborhood. Her front yard was arrayed with rows and rows of the most beautiful multiple-colored roses. Mary and I were quite taken by the splendid work she had accomplished on her entire front lawn. Our admiration was interrupted by a familiar voice.

"Hi you two, welcome to my Hollywood home." Jackie chirped.

After graciously welcoming us in, she ran for the sun-tea. Right away I noticed the exact same furniture that had adorned her old apartment and it was still too ostentatious for the size of her new home.

"Will she be moving again?" I thought to myself.

As Mary and I sat down, on her couch, I intently scouted the room. I could barely wait for Jackie to return. I couldn't wait to pop the question. Soon she was back with sun tea in hand and I stood-up and asked, "Where's Maurice?"

"Oh he spends most of his time living out back, in a cage." She nonchalantly, replied.

After noticing the astonished look on our faces she quickly retorted "Well that's because he has a wife and a family. Notable people have even adopted his children. I advertise them as "Star Bunnies."
Jackie took us out back to see "good old" Maurice and family. They were cute but the adoption price was way out of my league. We came back into the living room and gave her an update on our activities. She particularly showed a great interest in our Child Abuse Project.

Mary finally got around to asking Jackie the number one question, "What's happening with **WHITE CRACKER**, Jackie? It's been five years? Is Mary

Tyler Moore still interested?"

Jackie quickly responded, "Well, she gave it back to me...but I gave it to Carol Burnett. She's doing movies now you know."

I couldn't believe my ears. What a quick, comeback, creative answer and Jackie churned that one out, in record breaking time. However Mary halfheartedly accepted the news. She considered the fact that Jackie <u>did</u> live in Hollywood and in Hollywood anything was possible. But I knew Jackie... She was stalling.

During the drive back, Mary and I discussed putting on a big Child Abuse Concert in North Hollywood, at the Palomino Club, where Mary and I first met. With all the publicity we were receiving, we were sure to pack the place. The next day, bright and early, I received a phone call from Jackie. After informing her of our new plans and without delay, she said that she wanted to help. Both Mary and I were elated. Someone loved our new idea and wanted to help! This meant that our idea was a winner!

The next months were spent preparing for this major event. We secured the Palomino for a twelve-hour concert marathon, from noon to midnight. Flyers were posted and letters were sent out to a variety of entertainers including singers, actors, comedians, magicians, dancers, and instrumentalists. Press releases followed. The media was contacted including radio, TV magazines and newspapers. The response was tremendous. We had so many acts, that we had to turn people away and tell them to contact us the next time we did a show.

A month before the show, Jackie decided to host an outdoor barbecue, in which she invited some movie and TV celebrities and producers. As Don and I strolled up to Jackie's front door, it dawned on me that he had never been to Jackie's and had never met my old pal, Maurice. We barely knocked on the door, when it flew open. There stood Jackie locked arm-in-arm with a tall, dark handsome actor named Carl Strano, who had appeared on TV's **DYNASTY** and in the movie **DREAMSCAPE.**

"I'm his new manager." Jackie quickly announced.

"Okay," I thought. "First she kicks Maurice (the rabbit)outside in the cold then she dumps him, professionally, for some human actor. Maurice must be crushed."

Both Don and I were starved, considering we worked hard all day and skipped lunch...so we were scouting out the food, looking for the steaks. Through the house we wandered and onto the patio in the back yard. Easily, we recognized some of the celebrities standing around, from film and TV. It was exciting...but I wondered, "How come they weren't eating?

Well that's their problem...more food for us."

Undaunted by the Hollywood types Don and I continued our search for the steaks, but could find no grill. Then we noticed, in the middle of a picnic table, a large metal cooking pot (like the kind my mom would use to pluck the features off of a chicken). Don bravely looked into the pot and saw our meal. As he scooped up the ladle and filled our plastic bowls, we discovered a watery solution of canned whole kernel corn and pieces of boned chicken ...It was Jackie's barbecued chicken soup. The disappointment on our faces would have been worth a shot on the TV show, **AMERICA'S MOST FUNNIEST HOME VIDEOS**. With hunger pains still gnawing at our guts, we boldly dipped our plastic spoons into the soupy substance only to be hit with another surprise...the soup was cold. The only highlight of the evening was watching the celebrities and guests take their first bite of Jackie's cold, barbecued chicken soup...yummy.

By the time the concert date arrived, I was totally exhausted. That morning everyone pitched in and helped. Don along with his daughter, Kathy filled red, white and blue balloons with helium and housed them in a collapsible fishnet. The plan was to release the balloons during the grand finale of the show. Jackie counted the money at the door. Ticket donations were $10.00 a head. Mary greeted the people and handed them buttons that she had manufactured that read **"BEAT A DRUM NOT A CHILD"**. I was in charge of the entertainers and coordinating the show.

For a brief moment, I stood center stage and reflected back to my first appearance at the **Palomino**, and how Mary and I met by chance? Back then my life revolved around me and my music. Nothing else mattered. But Mary taught me to truly believe and trust in God. She set an example of how to care for others...by sharing the gifts that God gave you freely and unselfishly. This woman had altered my life for the better.

By noon, we were on our way. People poured in from everywhere. Band changes went smoothly. Hollywood Celebrities filled the room mingling with non-celebrities. I sang **MOMMA DON'T YOU LOVE ME.** Mary recited **THE LITTLE SEED** and **FOOTPRINTS**. A wide variety of acts known to the entertainment world were represented. Testimonials and awards were given. The response was overwhelming.

By the end of the evening we had a full house and were ready for our grand finale. Mary and Jackie joined me on the stage, as we each took turns thanking the people for their participation. Other singers and entertainers joined in as everyone stood and sang **LET THERE BE PEACE ON EARTH**. On the final note the balloons were to be released. I saw in my mind how spectacular this finale was going to be... watching patriotic balloons floating in the air and sailing out into the crowd. The moment arrived. We all sang the final words: **LET THERE BE PEACE ON EARTH AND LET IT BEGIN WITH ME.** Unassumingly, I turned around and examined the stage behind us and saw no balloons. "What happened?" I thought. "How disappointing...no balloons!"

Directly, afterwards, people rushed the stage, showering us with praise and adoration, for providing a fine show, for such a worthy cause. Finally it was over and an hour later, Don and I combed the stage doing our last minute equipment check, making sure nothing was left behind. We had just experienced a fourteen-hour, marathon show and we were dead tired. After all the equipment was safely packed away, I stood center stage and blatantly asked, "Don, why didn't you release the balloons?"

By the expression on his face, I could tell that I said something wrong. "Honey we did release the balloons!" He insisted, as he pointed his finger upward. There, stuck to the ceiling were over a hundred red, white and blue balloons. Don continued. "When we pulled on the fishnet bag, the balloons shot up to the ceiling, as if they had been shot out of a cannon!" I laughed until my sides hurt. I could <u>now</u> visualize all of us on stage hitting that final note while this red, white and blue blur quickly shot up behind us, and stuck onto the ceiling. "What the heck was that...?" people must have been asking themselves.

A week later, Mary called, wondering if I had heard from Jackie?

"No, I've been resting up from the big hoopla." I replied. "What's up?"

Mary's voice seemed a little perturbed. "I think she's avoiding me. When I called her last week and asked her how much money we brought in, she insisted that she hadn't had time to count it. Kathy this doesn't sound right to me."

I assured Mary that I'd check into it. Jackie gave me the same story, but suggested we meet for lunch, the following week. When I joined Jackie and Carl for lunch, I got absolutely nowhere. She went on about how we had to form a nonprofit organization and call it the Child Abuse Network (CA NETWORK), where she would be the treasurer and Don and I could be the president...

When I broke the news to Don, then to Mary, we all agreed that it wasn't going to work. There was this lack of communication. Even though we all seemed to support a good cause, not everyone wanted the same things. Mary and I wanted to donate money to help active Child Abuse Agencies. We were not sure of what Jackie wanted. So we parted our ways.

On numerous occasions, Mary called Jackie and asked her to return her book **WHITE CRACKER**...to no avail. I could see that Mary was pretty upset about this entire Jackie episode.

"We'll put together our own Child Abuse Organization and continue to help the agencies." I assured her. "We'll call it **Entertainers Against Child Abuse**, the **E.A.C.A.**" (*and I did.*)

After appearing on numerous local cable TV shows I had become familiar with some of the behind the scenes people. One lady stood out, far above the rest. Her name was Dona Sheppard. Through her assistance, I was able to launch my own cable TV show called **TOUCHING LIVES**. Also during this time Mary and I visited child abuse centers and shelters throughout Southern California and Nevada, continued performing at concerts and donating our proceeds to legitimate Child Abuse Agencies.

This kind of work took its toll on both of us. At every function, we found ourselves surrounded by adults, who had been abused when they were children, seeking help. It became more and more difficult for me to even sing the sad song. "I'm a mom." I thought. "How could any parent hurt their babies?" It made no sense to me at all.

Late one evening, while reading the local paper, I noticed an article that infuriated me. It read:

A 24-month-old child was beaten to death by her mother's live-in boyfriend. Detectives say that it was an act of discipline that went too far.

This article appeared, at the same time the entire country was cheering for a little girl, from Texas named Jessica, who was rescued from being trapped in a well. The murdered little girl from Bellflower, California's name was Jessica and the two little girls were even the exact same age.

I couldn't believe my eyes. How could beating a child to death, be misconstrued as "an act of discipline that went too far" by our sheriff's department? Were they becoming completely callous and indifferent to human suffering, especially the suffering of a small child? The same article appeared the next day in a different local paper. I called Mary and read her the words. She was appalled.

"We've got to do something about this!" She responded. "If we don't, than more children could be beaten to death, under the guise of "an act of discipline"."

I totally agreed. Something had to be done. My first call was to the County Sheriff's Department, where I voiced my feelings of disgust, over this article. Next I wrote articles to the surrounding newspapers. Then I learned when the boyfriend's hearing was going to be held and contacted Mary and other interested women, sending them press kits that included a copy of the newspaper article and a poem that I wrote entitle Two Jessicas.

TWO JESSICAS

There were two Jessicas of the same age
One Jessica fell and a well was her cage
The entire country came to her call
With hopes and prayers from one and all
We prayed, we watched this little girl's plight
As the small Texas town went from day to night
The people joined from all around
Together they pulled her from the ground
And happiness filled the Nation's air
For our one little Jessica was freed from her snare
But miles away from this happy town,
A Jessica in California could be found
Too small, too weak, too young to fight
She battled danger every night
With no one there to answer her call
No hopes, no prayers, no protection at all
Her mother slapped the child around

Her mother's boyfriend beat her to the ground

A tremendous sadness filled the air

For the one little Jessica... Did anyone care?

And in her crib her body died

But her spirit lives on, no one can hide

For the movie of the Jessica pulled from the well

Was filmed in the same town

Of the Jessica who couldn't tell...

About her abuse and of her living hell.

Kathy M. Hampton AKA Kathy Bee

On the day of the hearing, a group of twenty of us congregated at my office and made signs that read **CHILD ABUSE KILLS, KILLING IS NOT DISCIPLINE,** and of course Mary's **BEAT A DRUM NOT A CHILD.** Our next stop was the Bellflower Courthouse, where we quietly picketed on the sidewalks and front steps. Our signs said it all. While people drove by in their cars and honked their horns, showing their approval, I personally felt like I was attending the little girl's funeral... Our little group had become little Jessica's family, by showing that we truly cared. The local newspapers gladly covered the story **"Ladies Picket Child Abuser/Killer,** which, in turn made the prosecution thankful that we were there.

After everything was over, the boyfriend received the maximum sentence; the sheriff's detectives retracted their horrifying statement and little Jessica received some sort of justice, but Mary and I were drained. It became exceedingly difficult trying to shake the sadness that accompanied the relentless task, of fighting child abuse. Concurrently, we both hung up our posters and badges and began to work on happier projects.

11 WHO WROTE FOOTPRINTS?

My life was hectic. Don was very supportive of the kids and my career. He wanted to do everything in his power to help me to reach my goals. (My dream at the time was to have the #1 record on the Billboard Country Charts.) After reworking a peppy song that I had written called, **LET'S GO PARTY,** the single was released on **Lilac Record Label.** All summer, calls were made to radio stations, press packages and press releases were sent. I even flew to Nashville, TN and promoted the record at **Fan Fair**. Then in the fall of 1988, the song charted on all the national record charts including **Indie, Cashbox**, and even **Billboard**.

I was really relieved when things began to slow down. It gave me more time to spend with Don and the kids and my friends. During a trip to the local mall, while standing in a Hallmark store, eight-year-old, Karrie ran to me, jumping up and down holding a card in her hand.

"Mommy, mommy, this card has Mary's poem on it but somebody else is claiming to have written it!" She blurted out.

"No Karrie, other people make the cards and design the pictures, then add their names to the bottom. They're only claiming their artwork." I attempted to console her.

"No mommy! This lady is saying she wrote Mary's poem!" She insisted.

Immediately I took the card and there it was, **FOOTPRINTS IN THE SAND**, followed by the words, Authored by Margaret Fishback Powers. I was in shock. How dare someone else claim Mary's poem. How could she do this? Hallmark was even paying her. They were paying the wrong person.

As soon as we arrived home, I called Mary and told her about this latest discovery. She was in total disbelief.

"How can someone say they wrote my poem when I wrote it so long ago? Do you suppose there's been some sort of a mistake?   Maybe this lady read mine, then years later, subconsciously, wrote something like it?" Mary began to speculate.

"I don't know Mary, but I'm dropping this card in the mail to you as we speak." I replied.

A few days later Mary called and painfully acknowledged that she had received the card. "I've already sent out letters to Hallmark.   I don't understand how this could happen.   I even have my **FOOTPRINTS** copyright!" Mary painfully added.

"I hope they listen to you, Mary. In the meantime, I'm going to see what I can find out about Margaret Powers."

The more I searched, the more I found her name appearing on various gift items…so many that I began to collect them. Hallmark wasn't the only one paying her royalties. Lenox sold a statue of Jesus holding a child and Gorham sold jewelry.   These companies advertised their products nationally, in publications that included, Reader's Digest, The Parade Magazine, TV Guide and other major magazines.

My family and friends joined in the search. Close friend sent me a copy of Margaret Powers on videotape, when she appeared on **THE ROBERT SCHULLER SHOW** that was filmed at The Crystal Cathedral. As I watched her segment, it was difficult for me to comprehend how two self-proclaimed ministers, such as Margaret Powers and her husband Paul, could address a nation-wide, primarily Christian audience and announce that she was the author of **FOOTPRINTS IN THE SAND**. She even added that **FOOTPRINTS** wasn't the true title. She alleged that it was originally called **THE DREAM**.

I couldn't believe my eyes and ears. There stood this short, salt and peppered curly-haired lady, with large, dangling, golden earrings, shaped like feet, taking credit for Mary's God given work. I was totally insulted. At the end of her segment, Reverent Schuller announced that her book, **FOOTPRINTS** was being sold, in their gift store.

I wanted that book. I had to know more about this impostor. The following week my sister Louvicia mailed Margaret's **FOOTPRINTS** book to me from Ohio. Instinctively, she ordered it out of a Christian catalogue, week's prior to the broadcast. As soon as the book arrived, I read it from cover to cover.

At first, I found out more about Margaret and Paul Powers. They were Canadian citizens. She was once a schoolteacher, who was struck by lightning twice. Paul was a magician/preacher, who had encountered some run-ins with the authorities. At one time, they worked in a Christian distribution center...I instantly thought, "Yeah and they probably saw hundreds of copies of **FOOTPRINTS IN THE SAND** pass through their fingers, signed "AUTHOR UNKNOWN".

Then I began comparing Mary and Margaret's claims to **FOOTPRINTS**. Mary claims to have written **FOOTPRINTS IN THE SAND** in 1936 and saved her 1939 copy. Margaret claims to have written the poem in 1964 and that it was lost or stolen by a group of furniture movers, in 1980. I compared the two authors:

- I discovered Mary's 1939 copy in 1979.

- Recording artist Christy Lane recorded and released **FOOTPRINTS**, her version of the song in the early 80's and prior to that a man named Edgel Groves made his recording

- Margaret secured a U.S. Copyright on, a group of works, entitled **"From The Heart"** that included **FOOTPRINTS (THE DREAM)** in **1987.**

- In **1984** Mary secured a U.S. Copyright on the actual poem, title and all **FOOTPRINTS IN THE SAND.**

- Margaret maintained that she traveled with husband Paul as he entertained at state and county fairs on the circuit, in the United States, when Paul worked as a magician.

- In the 70's, I traveled the fair circuit with a musical group called The Flowers Family and spotted **FOOTPRINTS IN THE SAND** in almost every truck stop. How could Margaret and Paul Powers have missed seeing **FOOTPRINTS?** Like the rest of us traveling folks, they most likely ate at truck stops too.

- Mary confessed to have little education, dropping out of school by the age of 14 and to have been impoverished at the time she authored **FOOTPRINTS**. Margaret professed to be a highly educated teacher.

- A highly educated teacher/poet would more likely be knowledgeable about the Copyright laws than a poor, young high school dropout.

- Mary's original version of **FOOTPRINTS** varied very slightly to the version of **FOOTPRINTS** printed today. Margaret's version of **FOOTPRINTS** has numerous changes and alterations. Even her original title was not called **FOOTPRINTS** but **THE DREAM.**

I gave Mary updates on my progress, but only to a limited degree. I didn't want her to become overly distressed realizing that she was currently being plagued with personal problems. Her son had been borrowing money from her, promising to repay, but reneging on his promises. This had been going on for years.

One evening Mary called dreadfully upset, and crying, "I don't know what I'm going to do. My interest checks are getting lower and lower, while my son keeps borrowing more and more money. He always says he's going to pay me back, but he never has! He only calls when he wants money. Kathy if I keep this up, I'm going to go broke and be forced to live out on the streets. That's the thing I fear the most... I don't want to be homeless and hungry anymore!"

"Mary you've got to learn to say no. You can't afford to keep giving when you should be receiving." I tried to comfort and advise her. This was an immense weight riding on her shoulders. Her dwindling, limited, funds dictated that she move-out of her "dream" apartment, to a lesser place, in a seedier section of Las Vegas. Although she appeared to be happy there, I could tell that she wanted something better.

Also, during this time, Mary received phone calls and letters from people, informing her that **FOOTPRINTS** items were being sold with Margaret Powers' name on them. They even mailed her clippings from magazines and newspapers. Once again, she was put through the indignation of being accused of being a phony and a liar, compiled with the reality of watching her own funds dwindle, while someone else, an impostor, reaped her rewards.

"It's all starting again." Mary sadly commented one day. "When will people believe me? I'm not lying. I'm a descendant of Robert Louis Stevenson and I am the true author of **FOOTPRINTS IN THE SAND.**"

A few days later, I received a copy of the poem below in the mail:

I'M SORRY I'M OLD

Alone in my apartment, I don't drive anymore.

Sometimes I wait and wonder,

Where are the children that I bore?

I pay my rent my electric and gas, how do you rate me?

When I'm below third class, Some things are a necessity.

Forty dollars to last me, sometimes even less.

Are there twenty-eight days this month?

Or are there more or less?

I thank the Lord each morning,

Count my blessings one by one,

Sometimes I get pretty hungry,

Before the day is done.

The medicine I bought last week,

Medi-Cal didn't cover at all?

That will be a meal I'll miss.

I couldn't see well, when I had the fall.

I'm sorry I'm growing old,

A little food, I could really use.

I don't worry about time anymore.

Some of us are being abused.

A crust of bread in my crippled hand,

My cane is by my side.

Lord send someone who really cares,

So I can see outside.

Mary Zangare

Mary had too much on her plate, to worry about Margaret and Paul Powers. Again the woman who had given so much, to so many, was worrying about her bills and a place to stay.

"How sad," I thought. "The world borrowed **FOOTPRINTS** from Mary Stevenson and replaced her name with the title, Anonymous and Author Unknown. But worse, Mary was being robbed of her rightful claim and given a new title, liar, impostor, and cheat. God gave those words to Mary. She made handwritten copies and gave God's words to others. The title of "**FOOTPRINTS** by Anonymous" must be discontinued and replaced.

12 THE ELVIS CONNECTION

Mary loved to talk about Elvis. Like millions of other women, she loved Elvis Presley. In the early 70's, when Elvis played Las Vegas, Mary saved her money and took a bus to see him. She purchased records, photos, and magazines that featured him. It didn't matter, if someone was impersonating Elvis, she liked them too. When Elvis died in the late 70's, Mary said that she was devastated and remarked that it felt like a member of her family had died. She began writing poems about him and sending them to her friends. One of her friends, while touring Graceland, accidentally ran into Vernon Presley, and told him about Mary's Elvis poems. He stated that he'd like to read them. The lady couldn't wait to tell Mary.

In no time, Mary sent Vernon a multitude of her poems. The next thing she knew, she was on a bus to Graceland talking to Vernon Presley in person. He congratulated her for depicting his son in such a warm manner, then handed her a special Elvis keepsake. It was a little gold stature of Elvis on a record. Then Vernon posed for some pictures and Mary was on her way back to California.

Any movie or TV show that involved Elvis, Mary faithfully was aware of the date and time. In the late 80's and early 90's, a woman by the name of Gail Giorgio, from Gainesville, GA, published a book that started the rumor that Elvis was alive and in hiding. Mary was fascinated by this concept. She was thrilled thinking of the possibility that her hero Elvis could be hiding out somewhere, in small town, USA. One evening she called announcing that she had just returned from the taping of a TV show, hosted by Bill Bixby, filmed at the Imperial Palace.

"You remember him," she eagerly reported. **"The Hulk, The Courtship Of Eddy's Father**. Well, this lady, named Gail Giorgio was on this show and it was about Elvis faking his own death! Gail believes that he's still alive and she has the proof. He was a spy for the FBI, you know."

"I'm sorry that I missed the show. It must have been real interesting." I responded.

Mary continued, "Kathy, I liked Gail's eyes. There was something sincere about them. I'm going to write her and send her my Elvis poems."

Mary followed through on her promise and weeks later received a reply from Gail. A month later, Mary sent Gail poems, letters, pictures and a copy of her book **WHITE CRACKER**.

A short time later, Mary called, "I need a favor," she conveyed. "Gail's going to help me get my book **WHITE CRACKER** published. She's real interested in **FOOTPRINTS** and the sequel **AND YOU CARRIED ME**. She's going to let the world know that I wrote the poem…and I want you to write the song."

"I'd love to. When is all of this going to happen?" I inquired?

"Well, I don't know…but it's great isn't it? You and I are both, going to be famous together." The excitement in Mary's voice was immense as she proceeded. "Gail is already famous. She's a New York Times Best Selling Author, who's been on **Oprah, Larry King**, all the major talk shows."

"It sounds great Mary! Maybe this is your break! Maybe Gail will be able to let the world know about **FOOTPRINTS.** I'll start working on the song, right away. Let me know if you need anything else." I replied.

"Oh there is something else…Could you write Gail a letter and tell her about yourself, **MOMMA DON'T YOU LOVE ME** and how we met?" Mary meekly asked.

"Sure Mary, no problem!" I gladly obliged.

The next day I sent Gail a letter and some material. In no time, I received a press package and a letter from Gail, confirming that she was officially working with Mary. Gail claimed to be well connected and said that she believed that Mary was the author of **FOOTPRINTS.**

Over the years, I had learned that most projects take a great deal of time. After working on the music to **FOOTPRINTS** and **AND YOU CARRIED ME,** and writing the basic piano and vocal tracks, I filed in them away. My time was then diverted to my pet project of writing a new musical play called **THE CHRISTMAS TOYS.**

I still maintained my monthly visits to Mary's. Her efforts to conserve money showed in her empty icebox. I would scold her about not eating, and then fill the cupboards with groceries that I purchased. Then Mary would make us each a big Italian Submarine Sandwich.

She kept me updated on her progress with Gail either during those visits, by letters, or by phone. So far, Gail was sending letters out to publishing companies, trying to get a bite, and batting zero. This went on for months. One day, Mary called, and her voice was full of excitement.

"Kathy next week, my agent Stan Corwin and an important publisher from New York are flying to Las Vegas to meet with me about my book, except Gail wants to call it **FOOTPRINTS** instead of **WHITE CRACKER** and you know how much I like the name **WHITE CRACKER**."

"It sounds real important Mary. Take out all of your **FOOTPRINTS** items, the old 1939 poem, your copyright, and your newspaper clippings about Vietnam and have them laid out on the table, ready for them to examine. If they are as important as you say they are, then they don't have time to waste." I cautiously advised.

Mary answered in a yeah, sure, kind of manner. The tone in her voice told me that she was going to do this thing her way and that she did not need any of my help.

So I finally, bluntly come right about and asked, "Do you want me to fly to Las Vegas and be there with you, when those guys show up?"

There was a dead silence on the other end. In a very hostile voice she replied, "No, I can handle it myself. I'm a big girl and I'm fully capable of taking care of my own business."

Dead silence again. I broke the ice. "Okay Mary. But if you need me just call me. I just wanted to help you."

The next week, about 10 PM, a distraught, Mary was on the phone, "Kathy it was horrible. The agent, Stan and the New York publisher came to my house and started asking me all kinds of questions about **FOOTPRINTS**. You know how upset I get when I think about what's happened with it...I started to cry."

A whimpering sound was all that could be heard...then a full-blown wail.

"Mary, what happened? What's wrong?" I asked sympathetically.

After a few moments, she regained her composure, she then continued. "I made a big pot of spaghetti and a pot of coffee. I asked them to eat some dinner. They refused and commented that they were interested in the **FOOTPRINTS** poem, only. They wanted to know all these things; "Why didn't you get a copyright on it earlier? Show us the proof. How do we know you're really the author? How do we know you really wrote it in 1936?" All I could do was cry. Then they excused themselves and left. When I told Gail, she became so upset and said that I messed up a very important book deal."

"Next time Mary, Let me help." I urged.

"I will Kathy. I will!" She softly replied.

As I laid down the phone my mind began to travel back. I thought about the stories that Mary shared with me. It seemed that she was always getting into one conflict after another, but God always provided a way for her to overcome or escape. I could only imagine what she went through this evening. She was way too sensitive to handle the New York business types.

I walked outside. The Santa Ana winds were blowing a soft warm breeze, caressing me like a wondrous whispering friend. As my eyes gazed upward, into the star filled heavens, I softly prayed, "Lord please help Mary. She really needs you to carry her…again."

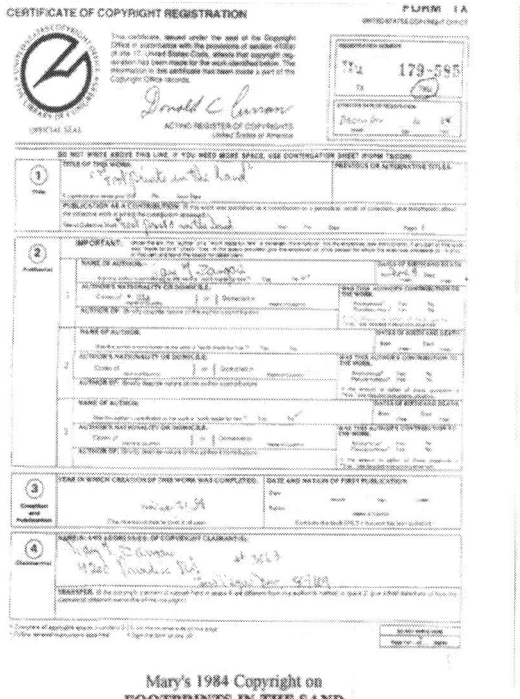

Mary's 1984 Copyright on
FOOTPRINTS IN THE SAND

13 A PROMISE FROM THE LORD

In the 80's, my numerous, visits to Nashville yielded some fruits. I was signed briefly to an independent record label, headed by Country Singer, Johnny Paycheck, until he went to jail. Then I worked with his manager, before he went to jail.

But the early 90's were quick pace. In 1992, I found myself in Branson, Missouri scouting theaters and meeting with Bobby Helms, of **JINGLE BELL ROCK** and **SPECIAL ANGEL** fame, to discuss a theater project in Myrtle Beach, SC. All went well and immediate plans were underway to relocate to Myrtle Beach. I was going to star in my very own theater called **"THE QUEEN BEE THEATER"**. Don was planning on selling the business and helping me with operations.

When I gave Mary the news, she was both happy and sad. I encouraged her to come-out and stay with us anytime…but when it came time to say goodbye, it felt like I would never see her again. We both held-on to each other and cried. Neither one of us wanted to let go. Fully aware of our emotional state, Don walked out of Mary's apartment, drove the car to the front, rolled down the window and yelled, "We really do have to go and right now! The bus is leaving!"

Myrtle Beach was a beautiful place, full of large pine trees and clean, white, sandy beaches that put California beaches to shame. The people were friendly and kind, especially, my band manager Dave Dewberry and his girlfriend Marilyn. I even found a spirit filled church, where I never missed a Sunday service. But the theater project was a nightmare. Bobby Helms' **SPECIAL ANGEL THEATER** was the only theater that was officially completed and opened. A month later, the project manager suddenly skipped town, taking along with him our future theatrical dreams.

For nine months I had resided in beautiful Myrtle Beach and now it was time for me to leave. Don drove the kids and I back to California, in record breaking time. In two days we went from Myrtle Beach, South Carolina to Bellflower, California, cross-country and celebrated Christmas at home.

It took a while to unpack and get settled in. I hated the fact that my dream of having my own theater had been wiped out but deep down I was happy to be back in California. I missed my friends and the freedom that only California could offer. The ocean was only fifteen minutes away and the mountains were a half-hour. You only 30 minutes away (depending on traffic) from a multitude of recording and movie studios and of course, there's the lovely almost perpetual summertime weather.

I thought it really odd that since I had been back, I hadn't heard from Mary. I would call her number and get no answer. Then early one Saturday morning the phone rang. It was Mary's younger sister Dot.

"Mary's in a coma and they're not expecting her to live. They've called all the family. Since you're her best friend, I thought you ought to know." Dot tearfully said.

Tears began streaming down my face, "What hospital is she in?" What's the number, oh my God?" I exclaimed as my heart beat faster.
Rapidly, I took down the number and contacted the hospital. Don was standing by watching me write down all the information on paper. After I

hung-up, I buried my head into Don's shoulder and began to wail. "I have to see Mary. I don't care if I'm not her family. I've got to see Mary."

Don promised that he would take me early the next morning. The five-hour ride was a solemn one. Memories of Mary and all of our experiences flooded my brain.

"God, I pleaded; I know that with Jesus' stripes we are healed. Please, heal Mary, please."

Upon entering Mary's room, in the Critical Care Ward, I was in disbelief. Mary's two-hundred-pound plus body had shrunk to a ninety-eight-pound helpless, weakling. Tubes protruded from everywhere. Machines monitored her every breath and heart beat.

"I'll let you two be alone," Don tenderly said.

"Honey," I interjected as he headed for the door. "Do you think they'll let me leave Mary my new cassette tape album?" *(The album was a Tribute To Patsy Cline produced by Lawton Jiles and Buster Beam.)*

I pulled the cassette out of my purse and handed it to him.

"I'll ask one of the nurses." He gently replied. A few minutes later the nurse returned with the cassette and a cassette player, with the tape already in it.

"I'll do you one better," the nurse said. "You can play the songs for Mary yourself."

The nurse smiled; handed the small cassette player to me and walked away, quietly shutting the door behind her. Through a large glass window, I noticed Don and the nurse carrying on a conversation. Although I couldn't hear what they were saying, it looked as though it was not good...terribly serious conversation.

I placed the cassette player on the edge of Mary's bed then pressed play. The music softly filled the air with my renditions of the song **PATSY, WE'RE STILL LOVIN'YOU**. As the music continued to play, I placed Mary's frail cold hand in mine and began to sing along with my own, recorded voice:

WE STILL GO OUT WALKIN' AFTER MIDNIGHT
AND LET THE TEARDROPS FALL WHEN WE'RE BLUE
SOMETIMES WE GO CRAZY AND STILL FALL TO PIECES
THEN HAVE SWEET DREAMS ABOUT YOU
YES PATSY WE'RE STILL LOVIN' YOU

All of a sudden, Mary's feet started moving. She was dancing to the music. Don and the nurse looked in through the window. Off ran the nurse, then she returned with the doctor. Suddenly, the room filled with people working on Mary. I politely asked, the nurse if I could leave the tape. She nodded in agreement then I left the room, and joined Don in the hall.

"What's going on? Why are they all excited?" I asked feeling quite bewildered.

"They're excited about Mary moving. That's a good sign!" He happily replied.

When we arrived home, later that evening, I heard an inner voice say, "Call Gail Giorgio." I thought it strange considering the fact that I had only spoken to her briefly, sometime in 1991. But I complied with my inner-self and called her giving her a complete update on Mary. Immediately, she explained how she had been trying to get in touch with Mary but after numerous attempts was unsuccessful.

"Now this explains it." She replied in an exhausted manner. Gail went on to explain how she had finally secured a contract with a publisher, for Mary's life story, **FOOTPRINTS**.

Once again, I explained to Gail, about Mary's critical condition.

"The only thing that we can do for Mary, right now, is to pray." I concluded.

The following day, Dot called with good news. "Mary is out of the coma and wants to go home." She gleefully remarked and the doctor says that she looks like she's completely out of the woods."

I was overwhelmed with joy. Mary was going to be okay! "Thank you Lord!" I yelled. Then I called everyone!

Gail sounded both troubled and relieved. Emphatically, she stressed that she had to get the publishing contract to Mary and that Mary would most likely need a manager. After fifteen minutes of explaining the "light" duties of an author and a manager, she asked if I would manage Mary.
At first I laughed. "Nobody can manage Mary. She's always been her own boss." I jokingly replied. But Gail sounded serious, even desperate.

"I've worked hard for three years and I don't want to watch all my efforts to go to waste. Besides, this is Mary's opportunity to re-claim her poem. It's her chance of a lifetime." Gail urged.

I assured Gail that I would talk it over with Don and get back with her. After what I had currently, experienced in Myrtle Beach, I was in no hurry to get involved with another strange personality or into any uncharted waters.

On a piece of paper, I wrote down the positive and negatives, pros and cons, of being Mary's manager, finding more cons than pros. The pluses were that I enjoyed deeply loved Mary and desperately wanted her to reclaim ownership of **Footprints In The Sand**.

Don strongly advised, "You're not getting involved into any kind of a deal without a written contract! People have burned you too many times. I won't see them take advantage of you again!"

After weighing it all out, I called Gail, and let her know that I would represent Mary, spelling out all of my contractual conditions. We also had been advised by Gail that Mary needed to have a Last Will and Testament.

Mary's rehab went well and soon she was home, facing the reality that losing 100 pounds is extremely devastating to your wardrobe. She had no clothes that fit. The only piece of clothing that she could wear was a hospital gown. Even her underwear hugged her ankles. As Mary's new manager, I went shopping and bought Mary an entire new wardrobe.

When we arrived at her front door, with bags in hand, she was totally surprised.

"Is it Christmas?" She immediately asked. Are all of these for me?"
We brought in the first bags then Don made more trips, down the wobbly stairs and out to the car to for the remainder of the clothes.

Her mode of transportation, these days was a walker and a wheelchair. I thought about how she loved to dance and wondered if she would ever be able to "shake a rug" again. Still she seemed happy…happy that somebody cared. This meant the world to her.

I informed Mary that she would need a Will. She agreed and we called our notary friends who lived in Las Vegas. Don and I both left the room when she filled out her Will and had it notarized.

Mary couldn't wait to tell me and (various reporters) about her near death experience. I sat there spellbound. I had often read articles and saw TV shows documenting people who shared those kind of experiences, but never dreamed that I would ever personally know someone, whom the doctors declared clinically dead, and had total recall of the place beyond.

"Why not Mary," I thought. "She had always been a highly spiritual person."

As Mary took a deep breath, she began, "All I knew was that I couldn't breathe, and then I was out. The doctor told me afterwards that I had experienced total respiratory failure and my heart had completely stopped. During the time that I blacked out, I opened my spiritual eyes and felt my inner person float up and out of my body. It was a feeling of both exhilaration and of complete freedom. Never once did I look back. There was a dark tunnel before me.

I longed to travel beyond the tunnel. Then unexpectedly, the darkness of the tunnel somehow engulfed me. A glorious bright light awaited me at the end of the tunnel. Sweet, musical voices beckoned me, calling me by name…"Mary, Mary," the voices pleasantly sang. Then my feet delicately landed on a billowy soft, cloud-like substance that felt like liquid silk, running between my toes. Then suddenly, miraculously, in a flash of wondrous light, standing directly in front of me was Jesus, who was gently petting a docile majestic lion, curled-up at His feet.

"Jesus, I'm so happy to see you. I'm so happy to be here"… He quickly interrupted me and said, "Mary you've got to go back…It is not your time."

"But Lord I don't want to leave. I love it here" I insisted.

"But you must." He answered.

Something was happening. My spirit felt much heavier. I involuntarily began to slowly move backward, towards the dark tunnel. "Lord, I yelled."I promise, when I go back, I'll tell everyone about you!"
Jesus replied. "I promise you Mary that everyone will know about you!"
In the blink of an eye, Jesus faded away. All of a sudden there appeared a beautiful black-haired lady, who looked like an angel, waving goodbye. Kathy, it was Patsy Cline!" Mary exclaimed.

In totally amazement I shared with Mary the fact that I was singing a Patsy Cline song to her and then she started moving her feet. "That's when you came out of your coma. And now Gail's going to tell your story. The world will <u>know</u> about you. Everyone will soon know that <u>you</u> wrote **FOOTPRINTS IN THE SAND**... Remember the Lord promised you!" I proclaimed.

When we were leaving Las Vegas we stopped at Whisky Pete's and decided to check out Mary's Will, which was in the trunk of the car. To my surprise and dismay...my friend Mary left everything to my husband Don. I was really taken aback and hurt. Little did I know then that this had actually been a good idea. Don, who had been a supporting cast member was now front, stage and center.

14 WHAT ARE FRIENDS FOR?

"No man is useless while he has a friend."
By Robert Louis Stevenson

Mary befriended Paul, a 74-year-old widower, who convinced her to move into a nice, big three-bedroom apartment, in a better neighborhood...with him. I tried to talk her out of it...but Mary was stubborn. On moving day, Mary and Paul failed to coordinate the actual moving dates. Her large furniture was left in the movers' van because their new apartment was still occupied.

With no furniture, Mary slept on the cold floor. To add to her distress, she had a life-long, cigarette smoking habit. Sometimes her lung capacity was not capable of accommodating her addictive vice. Right before Easter of 1995, Mary found herself, once again, in critical condition with total respiratory failure.

This time, Mary's sister Helen gave me the news. Late on a Saturday evening, Don and I drove to Las Vegas, spent the night in a hotel and saw Mary, early, the next day. She didn't look good. Once more, she was attached to machines but this time, Mary was fully awake and begging to leave. "Mary you've got to do what the doctor and nurses say, then they'll release you." I assured her. "By the way, did you get all of your kitchen-ware packed and moved?"

"Paul said that he was going to move all my personal things, little by little." She weakly replied in an agonizing tone.

For some reason, I couldn't picture a tiny, frail, 74-year-old man, carrying big boxes down two flights of wobbly stairs.

"Mary, we're going to need your house key." I said. "I have a feeling, that Paul didn't move all of your things."

She pointed to her little change purse and in it was her key. After assuring her that Don and I would soon return, we headed for the old apartment.
The landlady spotted us, saying she was glad that we were there. On Monday, she was going to take over the apartment and any items left behind would go into the trash. When Don and I opened the front door, a foul smell was in the air. The electricity had been shut off. To our dismay, the refrigerator was full of a variety of rotted and spoiled foods. Scattered throughout, the two-bedroom apartment, were Mary's personal things. There lay her hand written poems thrown all over the floor along with plaques, pictures and Basil's Flag from his casket. I was indignant over the disrespectful way Paul treated Mary's most cherished possessions.

Considering it was Sunday and getting dark, we weren't going to get a great deal of packing done and our kids had school the next day. So we packed what we could, shoved the boxes into my small car and headed over to Paul and Mary's new apartment. I could see Paul through his bedroom window, setting up his toy train set. After ten minutes of pounding on his front door and bedroom window, he finally answered.

"What do you want!" He rudely yelled in a gruff voice.

"Paul, I'm Kathy, Mary's friend. We've met before and this is my husband Don. We've been packing and here are some of Mary's things that we'd like to put in her bedroom."

"I don't want no more junk!" He roared and slammed the door, in our faces. "Well that old "Bleep, bleep!" Don shouted.

For a moment, we both stood there in silence and in disbelief. Then we slowly, walked away…realizing that we were stuck with a house-full of Mary's personal possessions.

We found a hotel, called the kids and called it an evening. The next day, we proceeded to get a truck, buy huge boxes and rent a storage unit. It took 38 big U-HAUL boxes and many trips up and down those wobbly stairs to secure Mary's personal belongings. After everything was secure, we said our good-byes to Mary, who had grown worse.

All the way home I prayed to God that He would once again carry her back to us. And once again, like a glorious reprieve, the next week, Mary was up and walking. That very same week, we received copies of Mary's book **FOOTPRINTS IN THE SAND**.

On Easter Morning, in the hospital recreational room, Don, Weston and I presented Mary with her life-story **FOOTPRINTS IN THE SAND** by Gail Giorgio. Her eyes lit up like stars, when she first saw the cover. Then she gazed sentimentally at every picture and made comments about the photos.

"There's Meet Arizona!" she said. "Ethel Waters lived down the street from us and taught me my manners." Tears formed in her eyes as she carefully ran her fingers over the picture of Basil.

Then I popped out my trusty cassette player and played Mary my newly recorded version of the song **FOOTPRINTS IN THE SAND**. She was elated.

"Oh my God, Kathy it's beautiful, Thank you and thank you, Don, you too Wes, I wouldn't leave you out." She laughed and cried at the same time.
We informed her about Paul's rudeness. She was totally surprised and had strong reservations about moving in with him. But was afraid that he might not let her retrieve her furniture, which was already in the new place. We also informed her that we rented a storage unit for her misplaced treasures.

"You two have done So much for me. How can I ever thank? She asked.

"What are friends for Mary?" I answered. "What are friends for?"
Mary proceeded to happily autograph books for everyone. Then she picked up a book and after closely examining the cover asked, "Why isn't my name on the cover with Gail's? I wrote **WHITE CRACKER**, and that's how she got my life story…from **WHITE CRACKER**. Gail and I were suppose to be 50/50 authors. So why isn't my name on the cover?"

I looked at the book and replied, "I don't know Mary. But I'll find out." I assured her.

The fact that Mary's **FOOTPRINTS** book had been released did not mean that people would automatically run out and buy it. Now came the hard work… including the press releases, radio interviews, phone calls and creative marketing.

"How can we let the public know more about Mary and the fact that she is the author of the famous poem **FOOTPRINTS IN THE SAND**?" was the question on everyone's minds… everyone that was except for Mary. All her life, she had worked long and hard and was finally able to celebrate the fact that her life story was in a book that openly stated "She was the true author of **FOOTPRINTS IN THE SAND**." It was time for her to enjoy some of the fruits of her own labor. Mary was thrilled when she received her advance royalty checks... one was for $1500.00. The contract dictated that Gail and Mary would each receive one quarter...24¢.

In 1994 the price of a postage stamp was 32¢. With every letter that I returned...money quickly went out the door, including the fact that: There was no internet; faxes and long distance telephone calls, were expensive, also considering the fact that Gail lived in Georgia, we had an agent in New York, another in Ohio, I lived in Southern California, we had an attorney in Georgia and Mary lived in Las Vegas.

Mary's health was still quite fragile. This did not affect her choice of maintaining her terrible smoking habit and going out to gamble in smoky environments. Her new roommate Paul puffed more cigarettes then Mary. With the doors and windows securely, tightly, fastened, the entire apartment smelled like an old smokestack. When I would explain to Mary what the smoke was doing to her body, she would reply, "I've been smoking all of my life and at my age, I'm not going to quit now!"

Soon, I found myself taking on the role of a mother hen. My Las Vegas trips and phone calls became more frequent. With each visit, I'd make sure that Mary's refrigerator was full. Part of my duties was to protect her from negative sources and only share with her the good news and positive feedback, so all communications from the public came through my office. I became guarded about the types of letters that came through the P. O. Box. I did not want Marguerite Powers or anyone else, to pressure and upset Mary.

Gail and I had been tediously working, sending out manuscripts and letters to everyone. I became a member of Women In Film and constantly pitched **FOOTPRINTS** as a Full Feature Film. Ultimately our efforts paid off. Two, movie option deals were on the table for Mary's life story. Marla Maples Trump (Gail's connection) out bid Single Sparks Productions (my connection). The following summer, Mary, Marla, Janie Elder (Marla's best friend and business associate) and I met at the Mirage Hotel in Las Vegas. What a memorable moment, it was for me, watching Mary and Marla swap show-biz stories. When Marla asked Mary about her old 1939 copy of **FOOTPRINTS**, Mary remarked.

"I don't know why you're so interested in that old worn-out piece of paper. Give me some clean paper and a pen and I'll make you a fresh copy."
I told Mary that the old copy was her proof. Mary said, "You keep the old poem...it's better off with you."

With all the publicity that followed Mary's claim to **FOOTPRINTS** began to receive greater attention.

One day, out of the blue I received a phone call from an attorney, stating that he represented Margaret Fishback Powers. He challenged that Mary Stevenson, my client was not the author of **FOOTPRINTS** and that we better stop making these false accusations. He even stated that he wanted to personally examine the 1939 copy of FOOTPRINTS. I informed him that I was well aware of whom he represented and that <u>she</u>, Margaret Fishback Powers was an <u>impostor</u>. Needless to say, he didn't like my attitude. Immediately, letters were sent to all parties, with the intent to scare people away from Mary's book.

Gail and I mailed letters to various companies, publishers, and ministries, informing them about Mary's rightful claim to FOOTPRINTS. Through my time and tremendous effort I was able to arrange for Gail to appear on QVC, to sell the book, the framed poem and the **FOOTPRINTS** pin and to inform the TV shoppers about Mary Stevenson.

Even Mary helped promote, by accepting an invitation from The International Soroptimist of Bellflower, CA. to attend their regional conference. This was her first public appearance. Not only was she their guest of honor, that evening, she received her first award for writing **FOOTPRINTS IN THE SAND**.

The program began with a half-hour musical tribute to Mary, in which I performed her favorite songs, including **BLUE BAYOU**. Then Mary (wheelchair and all) was lifted onto the stage. At that moment I sang my rendition of **FOOTPRINTS IN THE SAND** while holding her hand. Everyone looked on in awe as Mary too sang along, not missing a word. Next a short speech, followed by the presentation to Mary. The plaque read **THE SOROPTIMIST OUTSTANDING ACHIEVEMENT AWARD...**

Over two hundred Soroptimist representatives from various cities throughout the state of California, along with other state and local dignitaries gave Mary a well-deserved standing ovation.

"Remarks, remarks!" People yelled.

Mary took the microphone and with tears in her eyes, stood on her wobbly legs and quoted her poem, **"AND YOU CARRIED ME"**. Thunderous, applause, once again, filled the room. Then Julie Zelinskas, the president of Soroptimist, asked Mary to read **FOOTPRINTS IN THE SAND**.

As Mary read her famous poem, the room became reverently quiet. I looked on like a proud mother would, after her child had received a long awaited reward. I thought to myself, "God you brought Mary back to us for this moment in time. Watching her smile and seeing her tears of joy, truly has been a great blessing to me. This is what friends are for thank you God for this moment!"

In November of 1996, the phone rang. It was Dot and she was crying. "Mary is in critical condition. The doctors have called the family to her bedside. Mary's roommate Paul took her to the hospital and started acting like he was crazy. He began handing out money to everyone. So the guys in white coats took him away. Poor Mary…if you go and see her, can I ride to Las Vegas with you?"

I assured Dot that we would go together. My heart was in my stomach.

"Mary had to get better," I thought.

"We've got more promoting to do. The battle isn't over yet, because we haven't overcome!"

The next morning, I drove the long familiar five hours to the hospital in Las Vegas. Mary lay, sleeping peacefully, in a deep coma. Various machines, once again, recorded her vital signs. Her face and hands were swollen, triple in size. While Dot and I each, held one of her swollen hands, we softly sang to her the song **IN THE GARDEN**. Then a tiny tear began rolling down Mary's face.

"Was this a sign?" I wondered. "Does this mean she's going to be all right?" Her son flew in from New York and stayed with his ex-wife. With Mary in such bad condition, her apartment and her furniture had to be secured. A year ago, Don and I had taken on that responsibility, so this time I passed the baton to her son, who said that he couldn't stay, explaining how he had to return to New York and go to work. I pleaded with him to change his mind and take care of his mother's life-long possessions, but he refused.

The next day he was gone. He stayed a total of 2 ½ days, long enough to notarized paperwork, placing his ex in charge of Mary's belongings.
I was very disappointed "How could a son refused to help his own mother, when she's lying there in need?" I asked myself. "And where is the other son? Doesn't he care?"

Her sister Dot, a heavy smoker stayed at Mary's while I, being a nonsmoker, stayed at a hotel. The next day we filled my car with items that I <u>knew</u>, Mary would want and need, when she recovered (like clothes, her wheelchair, her poems, and pictures) then we headed back to California.

A week later, Mary was completely off the respirator and asking for a cup of coffee. While she was in the hospital, she developed a phobia about eating often fearing that she would choke on solid foods, so she totally refused to eat. The doctors proceeded to insert a food tube into her stomach. By January of 1997, she was transferred to a new location…a nursing home in Boulder City, Nevada right outside of Las Vegas. She was not happy there, feeling lonely and totally deserted.

Two months later, I received an unexpected, telephone call from Mary's apartment manager, requesting that I clear out the left over items in Mary's abandoned apartment. She said that she hated to throw away Mary's pictures, plaques and other personal things.

This time Don refused to help. All alone, I painfully made the agonizing trip to Las Vegas. As I traveled down the long desolate highway I began to ponder, "Where were all the people who said that they cared for Mary? Gail Giorgio wrote a book about her and never even met Mary? Her sons, friends, where were they? It's you and me God. Please be with me. Please carry Mary… and God carry me too."

When I arrived at the apartment, I was overwhelmed by the magnitude of furniture, clothing and papers thrown everywhere. I did not know where to begin…A voice said one cart at a time… As I began dumping the trash in the dumpster I noticed people rummaging through the trash. One man said that he knew a family who had nothing and needed furniture…Would I help. I let him know that I needed the day to go through everything and that when I finished that we could together clean out and clean-up the apartment. In my heart I knew that Mary would approve of this...giving to the needed was what she stood for her entire life.

Once again, I filled my car with things I thought Mary would want and cherish, and then I drove back to California... thinking, "What are friends for Mary? This is what true friends are for!

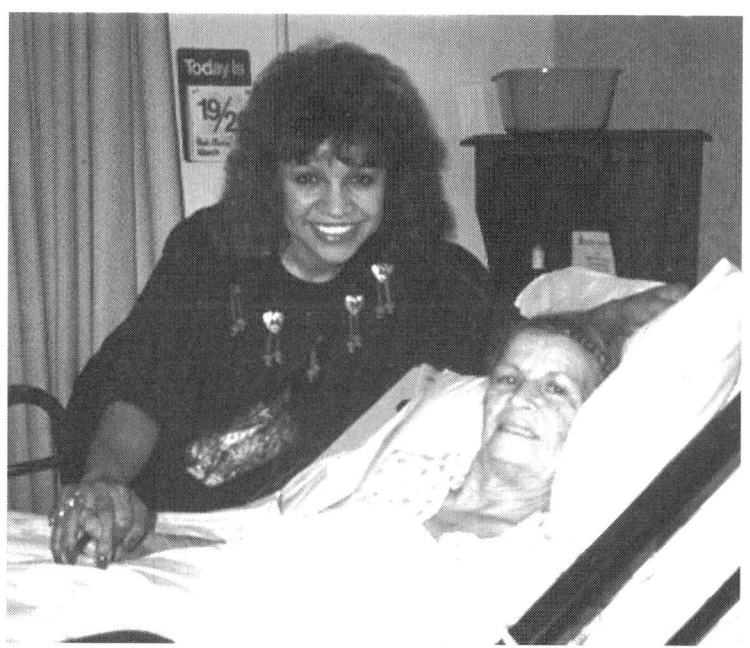

Kathy Bee & Mary Stevenson

15 REMEMBER ME

Margaret Powers' authorship claim to **FOOTPRINTS** hampered the movie project. Every time you'd pick up the newspaper, read a magazine, or the TV Guide, a Lenox and or Gorham advertisement, would appear, selling a Statue of Jesus or **FOOTPRINTS** jewelry. Included in the ad, were statements declaring that Margaret Powers was the author of **FOOTPRINTS IN THE SAND**. This made the Trump camp nervous. Everything boiled down to proof. We had to show proof that Mary was the true author <u>not</u> Margaret Powers.

Gail began to distance herself from the poem. She faxed letters to the Trumps stating that her book **FOOTPRINTS IN THE SAND** had nothing to do with the poem. The book was based solely on Mary's life. This meant that Don and I were left on our own to defend Mary. If we were <u>not</u> able to prove that **FOOTPRINTS** <u>was</u> Mary's, then there could be legal ramifications brought against her...charges of fraud.

I hired a copyright attorney to advise me on what steps to take. One of her suggestions was to collect older copies of **FOOTPRINTS** pre-dating 1964(The date that Margaret Powers alleged to have written the poem). So I contacted Chris Christensen a reporter at The Long Beach Press Telegram (A Southern California newspaper that has a readership of more than 100,000) and asked for her help. She ran a wonderful article, informing the people about Mary and her dilemma. The article also alerted others to the fact that we were seeking older copies of **FOOTPRINTS IN THE SAND**, predating 1964.

My phone rang off the hook. One lady stated that she received her 1st copy of **FOOTPRINTS**, from her adoptive parents, in the 1950's, however she couldn't locate the old copy. Another woman told me that she received her copy of **FOOTPRINTS** in 1960, when she was on a retreat hosted by the nuns of St. Margaret Mary's Catholic Church in Lomita, CA. A copy of **FOOTPRINT** was mimeographed on the back of a program sheet. The lady said that her elderly mother had saved the paper...But ultimately, she couldn't find her copy of **FOOTPRINTS** either. Out of fifty replies, no one could find their old copy of **FOOTPRINTS**. They had all, replaced their old copy, with a fresh new one. It dawned on me, that at one time, **FOOTPRINTS** had no monetary value. It belonged to everyone. Now, manufacturers had transformed the poem into a special, money making "keepsake".

Next, I hired, Native Californian, research journalist. In all of her thirty-plus years, she had never even heard of **FOOTPRINTS,** but was immediately moved by the inspirational words. Both of us searched the Internet, libraries, mortuaries, and church archives for anything that had been published about **FOOTPRINTS**, during the 60's and early 70's or prior. Through all of our efforts, we found nothing in print... nothing published.

When it felt like we were going to lose the battle, Marla's assistant, suggested that we have Mary's old 1939 copy of **FOOTPRINTS** tested (carbon dated). Even though we were extremely leery of trying this, Don and I both felt that something definitely had to be done. We had to prove, once and for all, **"WHO WROTE FOOTPRINTS"**!

Gail had the old 1939 Footprints copy that had been added in Mary's biography. When Mary mailed Gail the old copy, she mailed it regular mail, in a plain large envelope, not even insured. I needed to get the Footprints copy back. Gail insisted that I fly to Georgia and personally take it back to California. She was afraid that the old copy could get lost in the mail. I decided to immediately take a flight to Georgia to Gail's home. Gail had the poem encased in a trophy type glass plaque. When I examined the old copy, I was in shock... The glass covering had caused the light to drastically fade the words on the paper of the poem.

As soon as I got back to California, Don contacted his friend Long Beach Superior Court Judge Joe Di Loreto and asked him for the name of the "best" person he knew that could test the old **FOOTPRINTS** poem. He immediately said, "Call Kurt Schwalbe."

On Monday, April 28, 1997, I called forensic scientist, Kurt Schwalbe. Being one of the nation's leading forensic scientists, Kurt normally examined documents in high profile cases. This was quite a stretch for him… examining an old poem. His wife answered the phone and said that her husband was familiar with this case due to the fact that he only time he reads the newspaper is on his birthday and the article came out on his birthday! She said he remarked after reading the article that he would like to help these ladies.

One hour later, a tall distinguished looking, German born, Kurt Schwalbe arrived at my office, with over $250,000.00 worth of equipment. He quickly went to work setting up this elaborate equipment and arranging his tools.

"Well here it is." I said, as I nervously handed him **FOOTPRINTS**. "It's very fragile."

"I can see," he politely said. Right away, he began examining the poem. Then Don and Kurt carefully removed the poem from its enclosure. With great reverence and care, like a newborn baby, Kurt began examining the exposed **FOOTPRINTS** original. For two long hours he inspected samples of Mary's handwriting, from various sources, photographed it, then he used special lighting and techniques on the 1939 **FOOTPRINTS** poem. It was extremely nerve racking for me.

"Okay God," I prayed. "This is it... it is D-day!"

The silence was finally broken when Kurt announced, "It is definitely her handwriting and the paper is pre-World War II. I will give you a full report, which includes a review from my staff, in one week."

"Thank you God, Thank you Jesus!" I shouted.
I called everyone. Gail was excited and relieved. Our agents were happy. Janie and Marla were ecstatic. Even my mom and dad were thrilled. I felt like Don and I were "Rocky" and we had just won a prizefight.

Exactly one week later, Kurt handed us the full report, nicely contained in an impressive notebook. He explained, "In a court of law you normally need approximately four points to prove someone's handwriting as legitimate. As you will see, my colleges and I came up with eighty-four. The pencil that Mary used to write the poem was made out of lead. The use of lead in pencils was discontinued in the United States in the 1940's.

The paper that the poem was written on was purchased in Philadelphia in 1939.

Immediately, I mailed copies of the report to everyone. Next we followed–up and paid more money to have the **Footprints** copy preserved.

That weekend, we drove to Las Vegas and gave Mary the news.

"So they like my old poem. What's the big deal about that?" was her reply.

Although Mary did not like the idea of being placed in a nursing home, she understood that she needed the special care. One of the major problems with Mary being in Boulder City, she rarely had visitors and felt lonely and abandoned. The other problem was money. The cost of the nursing home was $4,200.00 per month and her personal funds were very limited. I could see that in no time, she would be completely drained of her financial resources.

The administrator of the care center ultimately told me that either someone take over Mary's personal finances, pay her bills and then apply for financial assistance on her behalf, or she would <u>have</u> to become a ward of the state of Nevada. Just the sound of my friend becoming a ward of the state, sounded like no one wanted her...This was not true!

I talked to her son about the situation, but he didn't want to help. He seemed to only be concerned about Mary's money. I called Gail and she said, "If I can get a buyer for my new book than I would gladly help Mary." To me, that meant the same thing, as saying, "If I win the <u>lottery</u>...then I'll help you."

Something had to be done, immediately. I discovered that Mary only had $15,000.00 left in her California bank and a much smaller amount in her Las Vegas account. Her unpaid, overdue, nursing home fees, alone, had already surpassed $10,000.00. Not counting her doctor and hospital bills. I hired a Las Vegas attorney and found out that Guardian Proceedings on Mary had not begun, but were about to commence in two weeks. This meant that Mary was two weeks away from being a ward of the State of Nevada.

My longtime friend Dona (from our Touching Lives cable TV show) and her new husband Jeffery Peters were extremely helpful. They had recently moved to Las Vegas. Dona carted me all over town and Jeffery gave me excellent advice. The plans were to bring Mary back to California. Mary loved the idea. I explained to her that I needed to be her Power of Attorney, because she had accumulated outstanding debts. She was in total agreement.

The idea of Mary moving back to California also thrilled Mary's sisters. With Dot being seventy-two and Helen eighty-four it was difficult for them, especially Helen, to travel back and forth to Las Vegas. This meant that they could visit Mary on a regular basis.

It took a week, but I found the perfect convalescent home. They had craft workshops, provided entertainment and each room had access to a patio area comprised of a lovely rose garden.

The next week Don and I flew to Las Vegas, chauffeured by Dona, picked up Mary and her bags and caught the plane back to L.A.X. Mary was thrilled by the entire excursion.

Immediately, she fell in love with her new home, her new friends and her fantastic new roommate, Irene. She even found a new boyfriend named John. Everyone there loved Mary and the best part was she only lived a mile away from me. We finally had the opportunity to go to shows, shopping and do lunch. Once again, our Mary was back!

While **FOOTPRINTS** and Mary's fame was increasing, the **FOOTPRINTS** book sales were decreasing. The book had run its course. Marla's movie deal did not transpire and Gail was frantically trying to resale the rights to the book. Although our new literary agent was doing working on it, there were no buyers. Rejection letters haunted us left and right.

The time had come for me to work on some new **FOOTPRINTS** ideas and to generate some positive income. The cost of lawyers, publicity, phone-calls; travel and Mary's personal care, plummeted Don and I well into the red. "When money comes in honey, Mary and I will repay you." I assured Don.

And then there was Mary. After all that she had been through, I couldn't stand by and let her name, once more, become anonymous. Most of her poems shared a common theme that said "**REMEMBER ME.**" That's what she wanted most, not to be forgotten.

Over the next months I worked on projects that promoted her name associated with the **FOOTPRINTS** poem. Mary even helped. She thoroughly enjoyed going places and once more, being in the spotlight. Wherever we went and whatever we did, she <u>always</u> gave God the glory.

A suggestion was made by our attorney that I get the **Footprints'** Story on the World Wide Web. So I enrolled in Internet school and created and established a **FOOTPRINTS** Website, which lead to our development of new **FOOTPRINTS** products including: tee shirts and bookmarks, all designed with Mary's name included as the author. I even paid for and attended various seminars and workshops that dealt with the subjects of publishing, promoting, public speaking and using better business skills.

One of the keynote speakers, at a seminar for authors, was our literary agent. When he went on a break, I had the opportunity to discuss with him my new ideas about **FOOTPRINTS** and how I was planning to license products bearing Mary's name. He loved the ideas. Then I asked him if he would represent Mary and myself, securing future licensing deals for the poem? He agreed. Naively, I shared my news with Gail.

Days later, Gail called, "I just spoke to Jeff and he had some great news! A large publisher is interested in publishing my new mini-biography (overview) about Mary, in an illustrated book of **FOOTPRINTS IN THE SAND**. Isn't that wonderful? Mary will finally get her wish. She's sure to become famous. I've done so much for her…the movie deal and the book deals. She's so fortunate."

Her words felt like a slap in the face. "Gail," I replied. "It has taken a great deal of time and effort, from many people, who have all helped Mary…"

"Oh I know that!" She interrupted. "But I've worked so hard and I've spent over $300,000.00 on this project. I've put so many of my other books on hold just to help Mary. But that's what this is all about isn't it… helping Mary?"

Gail insisted that we sign a written agreement. Then she immediately faxed me a copy of a proposal that she had already composed.

"I know that you're busy with Mary. She's been <u>so</u> sick and all. So I'll take care of the business end, while you help Mary." Gail cheerfully added.

A warning light went off in my head saying, "Watch out something's fishy." But I ignored that little inner voice. Was this the same little voice that got me into all of this mess, in the first place, in 1994 when it said "Call Gail"?

I thought that it was time to create a music video around my version of the **Footprints** song. I got together with some video tech professionals, my daughter Karrie and Mary who agreed to make this happen. So we loaded up the truck and headed to the beach...In no time we had the perfect scenery, sky and timing! Karrie played the part of the younger Mary walking along the beach...At the end of the video, Mary sat in her wheel chair staring out at the ocean. But Mary had her own different ending...She stood up and raised her hands up to the sky, while the camera circled her...then the chair was empty...

This was such a fantastic project and to this date has never been released. (It will surely be a big part of the Documentary **Footprints** Miracles Secrets & Lies.)

By the time fall came, Mary was healthier and very active. Oftentimes she would sign-up to go on bus outings and always join every activity. I had never seen her so happy. She had access to people, who openly told her, how much they appreciated her writing **FOOTPRINTS IN THE SAND**.

Even though I became very busy, I saw Mary at least once a week. I was working night and day, promoting an upcoming Big Band Concert with the

Al Sanada Seventeen-Piece Band, in which I was one of the featured singers. Mary was also going to be featured in the show. I planned on singing **FOOTPRINTS** and Mary was going to be the "guest of honor" at all three performances.

She shared the news with all of her friends. We supplied her with complimentary tickets, for her roommate, her sisters and other close friends, for the Saturday performance. All of the press releases that were mailed out to all of the local newspapers announced "Mary Stevenson, the author of **FOOTPRINTS IN THE SAND** will be honored with a musical salute".

In the middle of September, I received a fax from our agent. It was the contract from a large publishing house. With great anticipation I tore it from the fax machine and read the contents. Mary Stevenson's name was the only name on the contract. This was to be a book of her poetry...finally published along with Gail's overview about Mary's poems.

I thought, "There must be a big mistake. How come Gail's name was left off of the contract when she wrote the overview?"

I knew that Gail wasn't home, so I called the agent and asked him what was the deal? Why was Gail's name omitted from the contract, when she wrote part of the new book, the overview?

He quickly replied, "I told Gail months ago that we weren't using her overview."

I couldn't believe it. My little inner voice was right. Gail misrepresented the facts. I became angry and hurt. Immediately I called Gail and on her message phone and exclaimed, "Gail, how long did you know that they weren't using your overview? Call me, Kathy!" The next day, I was bombarded with ugly faxes, saying "How dare you question my integrity?"

With advice from our attorney, I instructed our agent to leave Mary's name solely on the contract and proceed with the deal. A month later, on Oct. 18th, I faxed Gail a brief, one page letter apprising her of our current situation and of the fact, that we could no longer work together. I further stated that any communications between us would have to take place through our agents and attorneys.

The following day, after Mary and I had just walked in my door, from attending a church service, a series of Gail's furious letters flew through my fax machine and onto my floor. I carefully explained to Mary what had transpired. Even though her health had greatly improved, I knew that she was far too fragile, to deal with this issue.

Gail's threats continued. In one of the faxes she even mentioned Mary's convalescent home. Immediately, I copied in the home and alerted them about Gail's vindictive behavior. She was acting like the wicked witch of the east, but instead of using a broom, she was using a typewriter and fax machine.

I deeply thought, "Mary enjoyed being at her convalescent home. This is her safe place, away from the cruelty of the world, where she was happy, respected and loved. Why would Gail, who claims to care about Mary, try to jeopardize her place of sanctuary? Mary never hurt anyone. All she ever did was give to others. And sometimes all she had to give was her poems.

Her life and her poems shared a common theme that basically said, "God Loves You by Mary Stevenson Zangare, a descendant of Robert Louis Stevenson, author of **FOOTPRINTS IN THE SAND.**

1997 newspaper article from the Press Telegram Mary & Kathy Bee

16 GOD SHE'S IN YOUR HANDS

Everyone was excited. Mary's 75th surprise birthday party would soon be underway. The recreational hall, at the nursing home was colorfully decorated with balloons and paper records, strung from the ceiling. Big band leader, Al Sanada, with his saxophone in hand, and wife Helen by his side patiently waited. One of Southern California's top vocalists Frank Wright was all warmed up and ready to sing. Mary's sisters Helen, Dot, and her niece Helen were anticipating Mary's arrival and what she would say. Bellflower Soroptimist members, including their president Jill Chapman and even the Mayor of Bellflower, Ruth Gilson plus Mary's closest friends from the nursing home were all awaiting her grand entrance.

As the videotape rolled, staff members wheeled Mary into the recreational hall, past throngs of well wishers. She looked like a queen and we were all her subjects. A beautiful new red suite, trimmed with gold buttons adorned her tiny body. The biggest, brightest smile spread across her face. As I walked up to her and gave her a hug she asked.

"Kathy, is this party for you?"

I laughingly replied, "No Mary this party is for you! It's your birthday."

"Oh my God," She cried out and immediately tears started streaming down her face. "In seventy-five years old and this is the first birthday party that I've ever had. Thank you all so much!" She repeated over and over as she dabbed her tears with a tissue.

Mary was wheeled over to a gigantic cake that depicted an ocean scene with "big" **FOOTPRINTS IN THE SAND**. Helen and Dot were by her side as people showered her with presents. Then Al provided soulful music on his sax playing Mary's very own **"SWEET GIORGIA BROWN"**. Next Frank's mellow rich voice filled the air with songs from The Platters, a medley of **ONLY YOU, REMEMBER WHEN, IT'S TWILIGHT TIME,** and ending with **SMOKE GET'S IN YOUR EYES**. Then I concluded the musical portion of the program with **BLUE BAYOU, CRAZY** and **FOOTPRINTS**. Bellflower's Mayor, Ruth Gilson, presented Mary with a certificate. Then Ray Smith, the administrator of the home, said warm, loving kind words about Mary. Afterwards he read one of Mary's poems that had become dear to him titled:

WHY DON'T THEY WANT US?

When we grow old they don't want us anymore
We raised them, gave them everything they wanted
On us they closed the door.
This is true my friend, it happens all the time
What good are we when we can't give them a dime?
Some of us may drool. Some may wet
They don't want us anymore. How soon they forget.
We may use a walker. Some of us use a cane
We are no longer fast and yet we feel the pain
We know that we are in the way.
There's nothing that we can do
So we must hold our tongue "Lord"
Till we come home to you

Mary Stevenson Zangare Dec. of Robert Louis Stevenson

People of all ages, young and old, wheelchair bound and upright had teary eyes. Mary's words had touched us all. Helen and Dot were called to the microphone, where they bestowed upon Mary words of praise. Then an elated Mary proudly, accepted the mike.

"I'd like to thank all of you for making this one of the best days of my life. I love you and may God bless you all." She then blew everyone kisses.

The party had been a complete success. After everyone left, Helen (Mary's niece) and I helped Mary with her gifts, neatly placing them in her room. Immediately I noticed a birthday card on her dresser. "That's odd," I thought. "I can't remember her sons ever sending her a card, whether it be Mother's Day or her birthday. Helen promptly handed Mary an envelope. "It's from Babe," she softly said.

The room became quiet. My mind went racing as I thought, "It's a birthday card from Babe...Mary's daughter." I knew that Mary felt us staring at her, as she slowly opened the card. Undaunted she silently mouthed the words, folded the card and placed it back into the envelope then sat it on her dresser. No words were spoken by anyone.

All of these years I thought that I knew everything about my friend Mary, but at that moment, I discovered something new. She had the courage and poise of a most respected queen. She harbored no regrets about the past. She didn't have time. She was too busy helping others. She looked to the future and helped others do the same.

The next day I came to visit Mary. I was puzzled when I found her lying on her bed at 11:00 AM. Mary was always "up and at em". When I would ask her a question she would answer with short curt replies.

"What's wrong," I thought. "Mary seemed extremely depressed.

Nothing I said or did brought her out of her funky mood. Her roommate Irene suggested that maybe Mary was pining over her boyfriend John moving out. So I figured that must be it. She was suffering from a broken heart.

I left Mary, feeling awfully low. While driving home, I said aloud, "God, I've done everything that I can think of to try and take care of Mary and make her happy. I've done all I can. God she's in Your hands. She's Your child." I couldn't shake the feeling that something was terribly wrong. The entire time, that Mary and I had been friends, she had never treated me so harshly and so cold. An hour later I drove back to the nursing home and saw Mary sitting outside all alone, puffing away on a cigarette. As I walked towards her I noticed many cigarette-butts in the nearby ashtray.

"Hey lady, do you want some company?" I boldly asked.

"Sure Kathy," She replied with a half-smile on her face. "Pull up a chair." She announced as she quickly put out her cigarette. Mary was well aware that I hated smoking and she tried to never smoke around me.

"Helen called and talked for quite a while." Mary continued. "First we talked about the party. Then she said that I'm lucky because I live in a nice place and that I have a good friend in Kathy Bee... She also said that you were responsible for putting together the party."

I put my head down and said, "I helped!"

"Thank you Kathy. I love you." She sweetly said.

We hugged and talked for about an hour. She was especially excited about the big band concert that was at the end of the month, on Thanksgiving Weekend. Then we discussed the weather, old times, and politics... Too soon it was time for me to go.

The nursing home had their annual Thanksgiving Dinner on the Friday before Thanksgiving and Mary invited me to be her dinner guest. When the evening arrived, I finished up the phone calls and computer work, and then rushed to Mary's. The recreation hall was full of people visiting friends and relatives. A pianist played old familiar tunes, while we were served a delicious turkey dinner. Mary refused to eat. One of the staff members said that Mary had stopped eating altogether. Something was so wrong. Although, she seemed to enjoy the music and playing her spoons, she acted very strangely. A cloud of depression encompassed her entire being. She wouldn't even crack a smile. I looked into her eyes and when she stared back at me, I detected great animosity. It was like Dr. Jekyll and Mr. Hyde.

Then for a few moments, the old Mary suddenly came back. "Kathy can you sing some songs for me?"

"Sure!" I instantly replied as I thought to myself, "Whatever is wrong between us... we still have music in common. She still likes hearing me sing." As I sang the words to the song **PEOPLE**, I looked into Mary's tired and weary face and noticed dark circles under her eyes. Although she didn't smile her lips mouthed every word to the song.

PEOPLE, PEOPLE WHO NEED PEOPLE
ARE THE LUCKIEST PEOPLE IN THE WORLD
WE'RE CHILDREN NEEDING OTHER CHILDREN
AND YET LETTING OUR GROWN-UP PRIDE
HIDE ALL THE NEED INSIDE
ACTING MORE LIKE CHILDREN THAN CHILDREN...

When the evening was over and it was time for me to leave Mary followed me outside in her wheelchair.

"Mary you have a cold and it's chilly and damp out here, in this night air. You don't even have on a sweater. The big show is next week and you don't want to get sick and miss it, do you? So you better go back inside." I strongly advised.

"I'm over twenty-one and I can do as I please. No one can make me do what I don't want to do!" She defiantly barked.

I knew from past experiences, when Mary had a bug up her nose, then you might as well let her work it out. So I got in my car and headed home...again saying God she's in your hands.

The following day, which was Saturday, Helen left a message on my machine at work, stating that Mary was in the hospital, suffering from total respiratory failure. I didn't pick up my message until Sunday. After church, Don and I went to see Mary. I prayed...and cried feeling totally helpless.

"Oh Lord, was I wrong to have brought Mary back to California. Why was she so unhappy? What did I do wrong?"

Don put his arms around me and comforted me saying, "Baby you were her best friend. You did all that you could for her. You faced <u>her</u> enemies and fought <u>her</u> battles. Now it's God's turn to carry her and you. You're <u>not</u> her God."

The next weekend, the Al Sanada Big Band Concert went on without Mary. It was one of the hardest shows that I had ever done. All the time I thought, Mary would have been so happy and proud. This was to be her night. But the show went on without her.

That evening, after everything was over I stayed up crying and agonizing over my friend. I loved her so much yet couldn't help her anymore. "Please carry me God, I cried, "Like you've carried Mary." I pleaded.

A few days later, Helen called and joyfully reported that Mary had pulled through! Once more she was back at the nursing home, but this time in an isolated room, due to a contagious infection. That evening, I ran to her side. Before entering her room, I had to put on gloves and a mask. As I slowly opened the door, I noticed that Mary was attached to I.V.s. Then she recognized me and she began talking away. It seemed like the old Mary was back. We laughed talked and sang **THERE'S NO BUSINESS LIKE SHOW BUSINESS**. Even though her feet and legs were covered with a blanket, I noticed that they were moving to the rhythm of the song. Then I broke out into a chorus of the old Kate Smith song **WHEN THE MOON COMES OVER THE MOUNTAIN.**

Mary abruptly stopped me, and began pointing her finger at a corner of the room, directly behind me, and said, "That woman sitting over there, in the blue sweater, keeps crying when you sing that."

A real eerie feeling came over me. "Mary," there's no one else in the room. We're alone."

"Can't you see her, Kathy? She's sitting right there."

She was insistent that we were not alone. I became fearful as chills covered my body.

"Mary, I've got to go know." I sorrowfully replied.

We had had such a good time and now something strange was taking over…something out of my control.

I took Mary by the hand and softly said. "I love you, Mary."

"I love you too kid!" She echoed.

The next day, when the phone rang, I was afraid to answer it. I felt like a yo-yo. But answer it I did and it was Helen. Mary's heart had stopped and they had to revive her. They hooked her up to the machines but she never came around. She was in a deep coma.

Getting through the week seemed like walking in a dream world. I would visit Mary, hold her hand and pray, then sing to her…but to no avail…there was no response. Depression was sweeping over me like an unwanted dust storm. I had to snap out of it…and soon!

My next project with Al Sanada was co-producing my musical **THE CHRISTMAS TOYS**. In the past, even though I was the author, I had starred in the piece, and worked on promotions but this year I would be the director. The show required a cast of at least twenty people, fully costumed, and well rehearsed. To meet those requirements, and in order to have a successful show, I (the director) had to display a very cheerful and positive attitude, considering I would be working with people ranging between the ages of six and sixty-five.

Then it was Show Time. The two musical performances were slated on the weekend before Christmas. With the help of Don, a fantastic cast and crew, I somehow made it through the shows. It felt good being around positive people conveying the message of love, sharing and caring, which was the theme of **THE CHRISTMAS TOYS**. Afterwards, I went to visit Mary, hoping for some good news, the week before she underwent a complete tracheotomy. This operation allowed her to be more efficiently attached to the respiratory. Painfully, I looked at my friend, who lay in total silence, with her head turned to one side and her tongue limply hanging out of her mouth. Towels had been placed underneath her head in order to catch the moisture that drooled from her opened mouth.

"God," I thought. "Look what man has accomplished. He can keep a lifeless body breathing on a machine. He must be pretty proud of himself?" I couldn't help but cry, thinking of the many good times we had shared.

"Mary," I softly scolded, "If you had just stayed inside, out of the cold night air. Why did you stop eating? Why were you so unhappy? Why were you so depressed? We have so many plans. Soon everyone will know that you wrote **FOOTPRINTS**... Come back Mary. I need you." I softly whispered.

There was no response. Not even a blink of the eye or a tear rolling down her face.

My entire world seemed to be doing a flip-flop. Mary lay in a coma and daughter Karrie, who was currently attending college, moved out on her own. Now I felt like I was being abandoned.

"Thank God for Weston and Don," I thought. "At least, they are providing some love and stability in my life."

A week later was Christmas. While the kids spent Christmas Day with Jim (Who some years ago remarried a lovely lady named Sabrina), Don and I decided to stay home, where I did something quite rare, "I cooked Christmas dinner". Later on that evening, after returning from a short walk around the block, I instinctively opened the mailbox. There before me was an official looking envelope. Immediately I opened it and found a court document, representing orders from Mary's son. The attorney's letter that accompanied the court order was filled with accusations, statements and demands:

Kathy Hampton is no longer to act as Mary Stevenson Zangare's Power of Attorney or manager. Kathy Hampton must hand over all of Mary Stevenson Zangare's possessions, including the old 1939 copy of

FOOTPRINTS to the attorneys. What it all boiled down to was Mary's son was appointed Mary's temporary conservator until a court date was established.

I was in totally shock. "I bet Gail Giorgio is behind this!" I said to Don. In the paperwork they kept referring to a confidential document. We were perplexed. That weekend we visited another attorney, who advised us to go to the courthouse in downtown Los Angeles, in order to obtain the remaining omitted documents. Considering it was the holidays and the fact that it was a Monday, the lines weren't as long and in no time we had the court documents in hand. Immediately I noticed that Gail Giorgio's name appeared on almost every page. To my dismay, I quickly discovered that she was blatantly falsely accusing me of misrepresenting Mary and absconding with her funds.

I thought to myself, "How could Gail, who is fully aware of the amount of time and money that both of us had spent on the **FOOTPRINTS** project, justify such allegations? I often spoke to her about the large amount of money that I had spent while Gail constantly made claims that her expenses well exceeded her incoming royalties. In one of Gail's many faxes she alleged that she had losses of approximately $300,000.00 in potential income.

In a total 3 ½ years that I had been Mary's manager approximately, $16,000.00 came in the door and $26,000.00 went out. Don and I paid $10,000.00 out of our own pockets, with the receipts to prove it. I received nothing but debts and now false accusations.

I was working on a contingency...someday basis. Now I was being slandered by Mary's estranged son and biographer, who were expecting me to become intimidated by their manipulation of the judicial system.

In this new court document, references were still being made to another confidential supplement document. I thought, "What could they have accused me of that would be so misconstrued, that would warrant a judge to appoint Mary's son, who lives in New York, to be Mary's conservator, considering the fact that she lived in California?"

In the mean time, I was still receiving nasty faxes and messages on my answering machine from Gail. One message Gail stated, "Kathy, I just received court papers from an attorney and I don't know what they mean. Call me right away so that I can get this thing straightened out, before it's too late."

More than ever, I refused to answer her calls. That woman was responsible for a tremendous amount of harassment and anxiety in my life. Then I began to ask myself, "Who was this Gail Giorgio? Why was she being so mean and hateful?" I wanted answers, so I decided to do a little research of my own and contacted a few of her former associates.

Almost everyone one of her former clients sang the same tune, "If you don't play by Gail's rules, then she'll slander your name. Beware, she's an extremely vicious person!" They also enlightened me to the fact, that Gail secretly taped telephone conversations.

Through the advice of one of Don's life-long friends, we hired another attorney, who (according to Don's buddy) was tops in his field, as well as familiar with the LA court system. Through his efforts, we obtained the final confidential supplement. Don and I both agreed that it read like a Gail Giorgio fictional novel, featuring me as her new villain. The verbiage included statements claiming that I had little to no involvement in Mary's business affairs, to too much involvement. I was accused of everything that you can imagine. The supplemental document was 2 ½" thick. Fortunately, I had saved every scrap of paper and was well able to defend myself against each of Gail's false statements as well as prove that she committed perjury in her court deposition. All I needed was a judge who would listen to my case.

Then came the worst part, included in Gail's deposition was a transcribed taped conversations between Mary and Gail. On the very day that I had faxed Gail the notice that her and I were longer working together, Gail, fully aware of Mary's fragile health, called Mary at the nursing home and carried on a series of lengthy, painful, hurtful conversations, with Mary. Gail's primary intentions of the sometimes hour-long interrogations were designed to destroy the long-standing friendship and trust that Mary and I had established over the years.

The following statements were taken from the actual confidential court document:

GAIL: "Um do you know that--did you know that Kathy's been collecting all your money?

MARY: "No, I didn't know that."

GAIL: "Did you know that you had, uh, signed a Power of Attorney with her?"

MARY: "Oh God."

GAIL: "Giving her the right to all of your money?"

MARY: "No, I didn't know that"

GAIL: "Do you know how much money I made for you this year?"

MARY: "What honey?"

GAIL: "Almost $20,000 dollars.

MARY: "Oh really?"

GAIL: "She had--"

MARY: "My sister was wondering about that.

GAIL: "Well, you know who has it?"

MARY: "Kathy."

GAIL: "Yeah, and you know how much more I'm makin' for you?"

MARY: "No, honey, I don't."

GAIL: "Another $40,000."

MARY: "Oh, God."

GAIL: "And you know where it's going?"

MARY: "Where?"

GAIL: "To Kathy."

MARY: "Why?"

GAIL: "Because she said you signed everything over to her with a Power of Attorney.

There are a total of 52 pages of Gail misleading and interrogating Mary. With every accusation Gail made, Mary replied, "Oh no Kathy wouldn't do that…or oh God." After Mary would speak, Gail would feed her additional hurtful lies. This brutal treatment of lies and deceit went on we suspect, for hours. Gail's twisted goal was to brainwash Mary into believing that her friend, "Kathy Bee" was a crook, thief, slanderer, a liar, and a total uncaring, greedy tyrant.

Being Mary's biographer, Gail was fully aware of Mary's deepest, darkest fears and that the fear of becoming homeless and destitute topped her list. Poor, frail Mary was now haunted by the terrible fears of the past…the fear of poverty. These under handed tactics, were used by Gail, in order to destroy Mary's faith and trust. Then she swore Mary to secrecy not even allowing her to discuss these issues with her two sisters.

Gail proceeded to contact Mary's son, filling his mind with promises of riches and fame. Instantly, he joined in with the charade of telephone calls. For a month and a half, since the 18th of October, until Mary went into a coma, she endured this kind of emotional torment and torture.

According to the documents, Gail had Mary swear <u>not</u> to discuss with me their conversations. Mary was <u>not</u> even allowed to mention that Gail called…there was to be total secrecy. No wonder she quit eating. No wonder she became depressed.

Mary and I saw each other at least once a week. Now, I could only imagine what she had been thinking, "Did my best friend, Kathy betray me? Did she sell my soul…for eleven pieces of silver?"

My heart sunk to its lowest. "Oh my God," I cried. "What have those evil people done to Mary?"

Feelings of both hurt and anger filled my soul Uncontrollable tears poured out of my eyes. "No wonder Mary had changed so drastically." I thought. "No wonder I saw hate instead of love in her eyes."

In total despair, I sought wisdom from my most trusted companion, my **King James Bible**, and turned to the Psalms of David and read.

Psalms 109:1-4

Hold not thy peace, O God of my praise.

For the mouth of the wicked and the mouth of the deceitful are opened against me: they have spoken against me with a lying tongue.

They compassed me about also with words of hatred; and fought against me without a cause.

For my love they are my adversaries: but I give myself unto prayer.

I then said a prayer, asking God to give me the strength that would be needed to fight my enemies.

Both Don and I knew that we were in for an ugly journey through the legal system. Trying to defend oneself, in this country, is not designed for the working man. The scales of justice are tipped by the amount of money that one has to contribute. It would take all that we had to combat this corrupt, evil enemy, overcome them and win.

"But Mary would fight for me," I thought "if the shoe were on the other foot!"

For 20 years, Mary and I shared a unique wonderful friendship no one could destroy. My journey through life with Mary had been a valuable, priceless, learning experience. She taught me so many wonderful things but most of all to trust in God.

TRUST IN GOD

Trust in God, when things around you look hopeless.

Call His name and He will always be there

Share His love with others around you

Open your heart and show people that you care.

For whatever lies beyond the next tomorrow

Be it sunshine or sorrow or pain

Trust in God to guide you to glory

For in His arms your will always remain.

Although I tried my very best, I was <u>not</u> able to shield Mary from this hurtful world. I could only hold her hand and grab some moments of laughter and happiness.

"Maybe a part of Mary wanted to believe <u>my</u> accusers," I thought. But in my heart, I believe that her inner voice constantly reminded her of the <u>real</u> truth, that I had been a true friend.

As for my own inner voice, my inner spirit was saying to me, "Mary's **Footprints** may no longer walk on the earth, but they will not be forgotten. God has lifted her up and He will carry her on to glory... She will live in the land of no tears and sorrow, with her father and mother, her sisters and brothers and her true love, her husband Basil. But best of all Mary will return to Jesus and He will say to her "My child a job well done."

Then I thought about the last words that I said to Mary, before she sank into a deep, sleep... I said, "I love you Mary."

And she replied, "I love you too kid." Those were not words of hatred but the ultimate words that one friend gives to another. Words from God... For God is love and pure love comes from God. Instantly, Mary's voice echoed in my head, "It's who ya know kid." I thought about it and laughed. She was absolutely right. For Mary knew the King of Kings, **Jesus Christ** and **He** always carried her.

Some would say that Mary and I met by chance; that I discovered her old 1939 copy of **FOOTPRINTS IN THE SAND** by chance; and that it was by chance that she became my mentor and I later became her manager. However, I believe God put us together for a reason... As for me... my life had changed. Before meeting Mary, my main focus was on me, myself and I. My journey with Mary taught me how to help others and share with them the truth that God is always with us, carrying us in times of great need. On January 6, 1999 Mary Stevenson Zangare passed away. Even though she is buried in an unmarked grave in Southern California, her work, memory and life will not remain anonymous, for her gift to the world was one of the greatest beloved treasures the world has known...the poem **FOOTPRINTS IN THE SAND**.

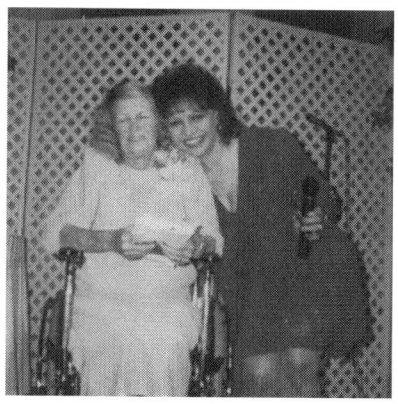

Mary Stevenson Zangare, a professed descendant of Robert Louis Stevenson, WHITE CRACKER, Stevey Richards, Grandma Marty and "Author Unknown"... is in **His** hands. For she is once more walking, along the beach with the Lord making...

FOOTPRINTS IN THE SAND.

THE EPILOGUE

It has been over 35 years since I first became involved with the **Footprints In The Sand** saga. Much has happened in my life; charting Billboard and Cashbox; winning awards; hosting and producing 250 TV shows called Touching Lives (Mary Stevenson was on the 1st show); producing music videos; CDs; writing & producing musicals; being there with Don Hampton while he was inducted into 2 separate Drag Racing Hall of Fames; watching Karrie's music career blossom as a background singer with Smokey Robinson as well as being an accomplished singer/songwriter; and Weston going to college and working for Boeing; to enjoying the weddings of both kids plus being a new grandmother. I'm even a Red Hat Mamma and I've produced 5 CDs & 2 DVDs for my Red Hat Sisters.

It's hard to believe that I am around the same age that Mary was when we first met. This fact and the recent suicides of celebrities, alerted me to the importance of the poem **Footprints In The Sand**. The need to tell my story and to share my journey with others has never been stronger. When I prayed about this, it was brought to mind that I should produce a documentary and call it **Footprints Miracles, Secrets & Lies.**

During my prayer time, the poem **Footsteps** was given to me. When I received this poem, I knew that I was ready to proceed. I share this with you in hopes that you will "Be Blessed & Be A Blessing"!

FOOTSTEPS

©2014 by Kathy M Hampton Aka Kathy Bee

AS I JOURNEY DAY BY DAY
ON THE PATH THAT IS BEFORE ME
THERE ARE SIGNS ALONG THE WAY
SOME GOOD SOME BAD THAT WARN ME

OF TRAVELERS WHO OFTEN STRAY
AND FALL INTO DESPAIR
WHEN THEY ARE LOST AND LONELY
AND THEY FEEL NOBODY CARES

OTHER SIGNS ALONG THE JOURNEY
SAY TO STOP AND LOOK AND PRAY
FOR TRAVELERS HAVE LEFT THEIR FOOTSTEPS
ALL ALONG THE WAY

THE FOOTSTEPS OF OUR DEAR LORD
INVENTORS, TEACHERS, DOCTORS TOO
HAVE ALL BEEN LEFT FOR OTHERS
TO DISCOVER AND PURSUE

FOLLOW IN THEIR FOOTSTEPS
THE SIGN READS LOUD AND CLEAR
FOR THOSE WHO CARED FOR OTHERS
HAVE LEFT THEIR FOOTSTEPS FOR YOU HERE

SO I ASK YOU MY FELLOW TRAVELER
BEFORE YOUR JOURNEY HERE IS THROUGH
WHAT KIND OF FOOTSTEPS WILL YOU LEAVE
FOR THOSE WHO FOLLOW YOU

ABOUT THE AUTHOR

 Kathy Bee is an author, producer of TV show and live events, TV host, musical playwright and an award winning singer, songwriter. Kathy Bee entertains throughout the U.S. opening for numerous celebrities including the late great, Bob Hope and Former President Bill Clinton. For ten years, Bee produced and hosted 250 TV shows called **Touching Lives** in Southern California promoting "People Helping People".

In 2012 and 2013 Bee produced the **Touching Lives TV Award Shows** honoring past and future guests who are amazing people...ordinary unsung heroes. Her current projects are **Footprints Miracles Secrets & Lies Documentary** and her new book **Footsteps My Journey**.

Keep in touch by going to www.FootprintsMiracles.com

The **Footprints In The Sand** song & **And You Carried Me** by Kathy Bee are available on CD at www.FootprintsMiracles.com/fpkb.html.

Be Blessed & Be A Blessing
Kathy Bee

Printed in Great Britain
by Amazon